smaller families
through
social and economic
progress

William Rich

 overseas development council   january 1973

The views expressed in this monograph are those of the author, and do not necessarily represent those of the Overseas Development Council, its directors, officers, or staff.

table of contents

acknowledgments

This monograph is the result of my year's research at the Overseas Development Council, made possible in part through a grant from the Population Council. The findings of this study of the differing effects of alternative patterns of development on motivation for smaller families have, I believe, immediate importance for decision makers in the related fields of development planning and population stabilization. The findings indicate that development which combines equitable distribution of jobs, income, and social services with economic growth has far more impact on the motivation for smaller families than has been generally assumed to date. They also demonstrate the need for, and potential profitability of, far more research on the relationship of specific aspects of the development process in different cultures to reduction of birth rates.

The initial direction for the project came from Lester Brown, Senior Fellow at the Overseas Development Council, and James P. Grant, ODC's President, both of whom continued their assistance through the last day of critical review. Several other staff members have also been very helpful—most notably John Sewell, Valeriana Kallab, and James Howe—all of whom made useful substantive and editorial suggestions. The first draft of this monograph was reviewed at an Overseas Development Council seminar attended by a number of economists and professional researchers in the population field. These participants were helpful in shaping the final course of my research.

A number of others have also given me thoughtful comments on drafts of this study. I would here like to express my thanks to David Sills of the Population Council, Professor Paul Schultz, University of Wisconsin, Professor Eva Mueller, University of Michigan, Professor Edward Mason of Harvard, Robert Shaw of the World Bank, Andrew Rice of the Society for International Development, Lawrence Kegan of the Population Crisis Committee, Raymond Ravenholt, Gordon Donald, and John Ratcliff of the Agency for International Development, and Professors Harrison Brown and Alan Sweezy of the California Institute of Technology. I should stress, however, in connection with these acknowledgments of appreciation for the comments and helpful criticism extended, that I take responsibility for the conclusions derived from this study into the still under-researched field of the effect of development on population growth.

William Rich
Associate Fellow
Overseas Development Council

January 1973

introduction

Continued high birth rates together with a dramatic reduction in
death rates have resulted in extremely rapid population growth in
most of the world's less developed countries. Internationally, this
population explosion has helped to maintain the great disparity
between the standards of living in the rich and poor nations. On
the national level, it has increased domestic pressure on governments for more jobs and better educational and health services, as
well as for structural changes to bring about a more equal distribution of national income.

The combined pressures of poverty and rapid population
growth in the developing countries are of course intensely felt at
the family and individual levels. Families living without adequate
food, education, employment, or health care have little future
security. Despite the major reduction in death rates in the past
two decades, many parents in the less developed countries still
perceive—often rightly so—that having many children is advanta-
geous for them, both for immediate economic and social reasons
and because of the persisting risk that offspring will not survive to
adulthood. This conviction sustains high birth rates in those countries where extreme poverty is prevalent.

The crucial question, therefore, is how the great majority of
families can break out of this vicious circle. Family planning programs have been initiated to increase access to improved means of
limiting family size, but other efforts are also necessary if population growth rates are to be stabilized within an acceptable time
frame. If developing countries are to escape the threats posed by
rapid population growth, more families must acquire the *motivation* to limit births, not only be provided with the means to do so.
*The evidence in this monograph indicates that policies combining
economic growth, more equitable distribution of the economic
and social benefits of progress, and easy access to family planning
services can bring about a much greater reduction in fertility than
can any one of these factors alone.*

Certainly the introduction of modern contraceptives in societies where they were previously not available has had important

effects on reducing births in many societies, since it has made it possible for those who already desired to have fewer children to limit family size with greater ease and certainty of success. But the emphasis of this study is on the need to recognize that, to tackle the problems of population growth with any assurance of achieving population stabilization, it is necessary to increase the motivation for smaller families. This in turn leads to the basic problem of poverty. High fertility is, after all, only one symptom (and one continuing cause) of the central problem of the poor countries; the real disease is poverty itself. Other symptoms of course include illiteracy, malnutrition, poor health, and unemployment—all of which may be exacerbated by existing economic and social institutions. In most poor countries, large-scale fertility declines cannot be expected until the living conditions of the majority of the population improve enough so that they no longer consider large families necessary for *economic* reasons and are therefore more likely to want fewer children.

To say this is not at all to deny the importance of continuing to step up both the provision of family planning services in most if not all countries, and research to improve birth control techniques. Nothing in this monograph should be construed as advocating reduced support for family planning assistance. Much more support is in fact required. However, it should at the same time be recognized that, in many cases, high initial acceptance rates of family planning reflect the tremendous initial lag in the provision of these services where demand already existed for more modern methods of birth control to replace cruder and frequently more dangerous means, such as abortion. The numbers of those who resort to birth control assistance should not be expected to continue to increase at the same dramatic rate once this pre-existing demand has been met. In the long run, hand in hand with family planning efforts, there must also be far greater support for those social and economic measures that will encourage the greatest possible numbers of families to want fewer children. The role of motivation is central to any attempt to stabilize population growth.

Demographers have long known that with sufficient economic progress, high birth rates fall sharply. The experience of Europe and North America over the past century amply demonstrated the change in birth rates that results from such progress. But since that reduction in births occurred over a long period of time and often at relatively high income levels, it seemed to have little or no relevance for most of today's less developed countries, where the majority of the population still lives in extreme poverty.

There is, however, striking new evidence that in an increasing number of poor countries (as well as in some regions within countries), birth rates have dropped sharply *despite* relatively low per capita income and *despite* the absence or relative newness of family planning programs. The examination of these cases in this monograph reveals a common factor. The countries in which this has happened are those in which the broadest spectrum of the population has shared in the economic and social benefits of significant national progress to a far greater degree than in most poor countries—or in most Western countries during their comparable periods of development. Family planning programs generally have been much more successful in those countries where increases in output of goods and social services have been distributed in such a way that they improved the way of life for a substantial majority of the population rather than just for a small minority.

The record also shows that those countries which continue to sustain high rates of population growth despite their achievement of relatively high per capita income figures have wide disparities in income and limited access to social services. Only a small group within these countries has started to practice fertility control; this group generally consists of the favored minority that has benefited most from the modern social and economic system. The remainder of the society—those living at, or close to, the subsistence level— accounts for the high average birth rate.

Thus a growing body of evidence indicates that a stepped up rate of production, greater economic and social justice, and a lower rate of population growth can be mutually reinforcing policy goals. This is not to suggest that the problems of the developing countries can be solved through across-the-board application of any single socio-economic formula. However, experience and observation do show that some countries have found an appropriate mix of policies that can simultaneously improve the economic and social well-being of the society at large, accelerate economic growth, and curtail the birth rate.

Much of the interest in the relationship between development and population growth has resulted from alarm at current high rates of population growth. Researchers initially focused on finding the most direct and effective policies to limit births—such as better contraceptives, improved distribution, and direct incentive schemes—to the neglect of other aspects of development programs, which appeared to offer a less immediate impact on the population predicament. It even has been argued with great conviction and urgency that population growth must be slowed *before* the welfare of much of the world's population can be improved significantly. Yet there is now evidence that the very strategies that bring about the greatest improvement in the welfare of the entire population are also the ones with the greatest long-term effect on reducing population growth.

Governments of less-developed countries clearly spend a preponderant share of domestic funds on education, health care, agricultural and industrial development—on social and economic policies intended to improve various aspects of the welfare of the population and understood in the broad sense as "development policies." If, as this study indicates, the indirect effect of some of these policies may, over time, have a great cumulative impact on population growth, then far more attention needs to be paid by researchers and policy-makers to the effect on fertility of alternative development policies.

This study of development and population growth is written from the perspective of development efforts *as a whole*, and views family planning programs as only one factor in that totality. Beginning with a survey of the correlation between development variables and fertility, the study examines various combinations of development policies that can lead to reductions in births, and discusses the role of family planning programs within this broad conceptual framework. A final chapter considers the implications of these observations for the policies of the United States and of other rich nations.

4

socio-economic progress and motivation for smaller families

Prior to the development of modern public health, sanitation, and education, both birth and death rates are generally high. The combination of high average infant and child mortality rates and a low average life expectancy makes high birth rates necessary for the survival of the traditional family. Under such conditions, population grows only slowly, if at all. As nutrition and sanitation improve, however, the death rate falls while the birth rate remains high, causing a "population explosion." But as living conditions improve further, the birth rate and, consequently, the rate of population growth, also fall.

5

FIGURE 1

The Population Explosion

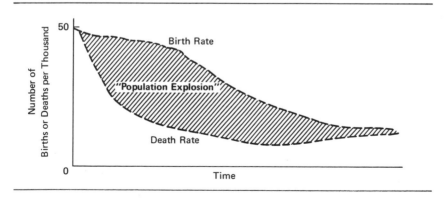

This theory of "the demographic transition" from high to low fertility, first elaborated over forty years ago to describe the demographic history of Europe, provides a useful introduction to the relationship between development and population growth. Various efforts have since been made to apply the theory to the modernization processes of all nations. According to one description, the entire world is in the grip of the demographic transition:

"there is no major population on earth that has not entered upon or already passed through the early stages of this process. As yet there are only two or three major populations on earth that may be said to have entirely completed it."[1]

Since death rates have dropped much faster in the less developed countries than they did either in Europe or in the United States while birth rates have remained high, the population explosion in these countries has been far greater. In the West, throughout an extended period of industrialization, national rates of natural increase seldom rose above 1 per cent, and the population doubled only every 70 years. In contrast, the average rate of population growth in the developing countries is now approximately 2.6 per cent annually, which means a doubling in only 27 years.

It was first suggested more than a decade ago that in the poor countries the demographic transition would follow a substantially different course than it had taken in the U.S. and in Europe.[2] This prediction has been borne out by the first stage of the transition in the developing countries. Some optimistic studies now also suggest that birth rates in these countries might in the future drop almost as quickly as death rates have in recent years.[3]

THE THRESHOLD HYPOTHESIS

The theory of the demographic transition laid the groundwork for understanding the relationship between development and fertility. It made it possible to view fertility and socio-economic development within individual societies from a common historical perspective.

In the early 1960s, the United Nations Secretariat took a further step in this area of research. It tested the theory of the demographic transition by conducting an extensive study of the correlation between fertility and various indicators of social and economic well-being. This work resulted in the formulation of the "threshold" hypothesis to describe the role of economic and social development in bringing about the demographic transition from high to low fertility. According to this hypothesis,

> in a developing country where fertility is initially high, improving economic and social conditions is likely to have little if any effect on fertility until a certain economic and social level is reached; but once that level is achieved, fertility is likely to enter a decided decline and to continue downward until it is again stabilized on a much lower plane.[4]

Table 1 shows the correlation between fertility and various indicators of socio-economic development. This data—presented as part of the findings of the United Nations study mentioned above—gives an indication of the relationship between development and family size on an international scale. The gross reproduction rate is an indicator of the average number of daughters born per woman of reproductive age (15 to 49 years). Thus a gross reproduction rate of 2.0 signifies that, on the average, each woman of reproductive age will bear two daughters if she follows the prevailing fertility pattern. Any level over 1 indicates that parents are being more than replaced by their children.[5] According to the findings of the U.N. study, when the various development indicators are at their worst (Level I) the gross reproduction rate is

TABLE 1

Unweighted Average Gross Reproduction Rates of Countries at Six Levels of Economic and Social Well-Being[a]

Indicator	Level I	Level II	Level III	Level IV	Level V	Level VI
Income per head	2.94	2.94	2.45	2.28	1.66	1.40
Energy consumption	2.92	3.03	2.34	1.78	1.72	1.40
Urbanization	3.04	2.82	2.48	1.94	1.31	1.79
Non-agricultural activities	3.04	2.99	2.21	2.03	1.55	1.62
Hospital beds	3.06	2.92	2.77	2.02	1.61	1.53
Life expectancy[b]	2.91	2.74	2.29	1.32	1.63	1.34
Infant mortality	2.80	2.66	1.88	1.63	1.63	1.33
Early marriage	2.92	2.91	2.30	1.55	1.29	1.50
Female literacy	2.98	2.99	2.57	2.31	1.34	1.46
Newspaper circulation	2.95	3.04	2.67	1.56	1.55	1.34
Radio receivers	2.94	3.04	2.82	2.02	1.58	1.32
Cinema attendance	2.98	2.76	1.89	1.94	1.52	1.81
Unweighted average of twelve indicators	2.96	2.90	2.39	1.86	1.53	1.49

[a] In this adapted version of the table, Level I represents the lowest social and economic level, and Level VI the highest.
[b] Developing countries are under-represented in the data for this indicator.

SOURCE: Adapted from United Nations, *Population Bulletin 7*, 1963, p. 144 (published in 1965).

7

highest; when the indicators are best (Level VI) the gross reproduction rate is lowest. The "threshold" concept described by the
United Nations study referred in a general way to the marked
decline in fertility observed between Levels III and IV.

There are wide variations in the national figures compiled so
far on the correlation between any given social or economic variable and fertility. Efforts to describe this correlation have been
made in many studies of virtually every area of the world, but the
quality of the data available varies greatly.[6] Given that qualification about the results obtained, two general observations can be
offered on the basis of the studies conducted so far: 1) the national "demographic transition" from high to low birth rates par-
allels the "modernization process;" and 2) within nations, the families having higher socio-economic status are the most likely to
limit births.

Several unsuccessful efforts have been made to tie down specific "cause-and-effect" relationships to identify in more explicit
terms the "socio-economic threshold" that was originally described in the 1963 United Nations study. For instance, Ansley
Coale, examining the statistical record for Europe, has found little
evidence to confirm "the existence of an association between the
beginning of the fertility decline and any specific level, or threshold, of economic or social development."[7] Paul Schultz, looking
at a variety of less developed countries, has noted that declining
births are associated with rising female education, employment of
women, declines in child mortality, and the propensity of parents
to withdraw children from the labor force and to send them to
school. However, Schultz and others do not consider the rudimentary data available sufficient to express the "threshold hypothesis"
in quantitative terms.[8]

There are no "magic numbers"—no precise literacy or mortality rates, or income levels—to mark any simple, easily identifiable
socio-economic "threshold" at which a family's motivation shifts
toward having fewer children. The evidence does, however, suggest
the existence of a more complex measurable relationship between
development and the reduction in birth rates. Although this relationship cannot be expressed in terms of any precise mathematical
formula and its results may vary between countries depending on
cultural and other environmental factors, its general shape can be
described.

FROM "THRESHOLD" TO "CONTINUUM"

Much of the skepticism expressed about any simple threshold
hypothesis is due to the marked *variations* observed in the demographic histories of different countries. In the United States,
changes in fertility occurred slowly and at relatively high income
levels. In Korea, Ceylon, and Taiwan, birth rates began to drop
while income levels were still under $200 per capita. In China, the
same may be occurring on a massive scale at even lower income
levels.

It is essential to emphasize, however, that the comparative
demographic histories of many countries also reveal striking *similarities*, and that this is particularly true of the most recent national
experiences of declining fertility. In the three countries men-

tioned, birth rates declined at the same time that the majority of the population appeared to have gained access to some combination of relatively modern social services and economic opportunities. There are of course no simple "country examples," just as no single factor fully accounts for a national fertility pattern. But recent fertility declines have been correlated with the distribution of socio-economic improvements in Taiwan, China, South Korea, Singapore, Barbados, Mauritius, Hong Kong, Uruguay, Costa Rica, and Ceylon; in the Punjab in India; and in parts of Egypt.

The experience of these countries and areas will be analyzed further throughout this study. The evidence examined shows that in every nation where modern goods and services have been distributed to reach a large majority of the population, national birth rates have declined significantly; moreover, in most instances, the decline started before the introduction of large-scale family planning programs, which then served to facilitate the continued decline in birth rates. In contrast, in virtually all of the less developed nations where such a broad distribution has *not* taken place—regardless of the country's total "wealth," its economic growth rate, or even the existence of family planning programs—birth rates remain high. Venezuela and Mexico illustrate the persistence of high birth rates in circumstances where the benefits of rapid national economic growth have not been widely distributed.

An hypothesis of fertility decline consistent with these observations does not imply that any one specific level of socio-economic development has special significance. The shift in attitude toward reduced births is, rather, a function of a combination of environmental changes that affect the orientation of families enough to alter fertility decisions. In a developing country, this appears to occur when families begin to participate significantly in the modern social, political, and economic system. Thus nations in which only a small elite constitutes the modern sector of the country while the majority of the population continues to live at the subsistence level and to maintain its traditional way of life are not likely to experience reduced national fertility as readily as those countries which bring about mass participation in the development process.

Nor does the decision of a family to limit births necessarily mean resort to modern birth control techniques. Birth limitation practices of many kinds have long been available in all societies. Late marriage, sex taboos, or long periods of lactation to delay new pregnancies all have the effect of limiting births. Parents may decide to limit future births after their second child, or they may wait to do so until after they have had five or six children. When a couple decides to prevent new births, it may consider such traditional methods of birth control sufficiently effective. A strong determination to limit family size or the experience of failure with the use of traditional methods may lead couples to resort to abortion or to the use of more effective modern contraceptives. Thus there is a wide range of possible fertility behavior, and any shift within this range can result in reduced births.

In studying the fertility behavior of a *society as a whole*, it is useful to think in terms of a "continuum" of fertility behavior. The distribution of goods or services among the population of a particular society can also be viewed in terms of such a continuum. Thus, a range in family size can be broadly related to ranges in education, income, access to health care, and other variables. A shift in the development-fertility continuum occurs when an increase in the volume and an improvement in the distribution of goods and services concurrently lead to a reduction in desired family size. According to this hypothesis, when a large majority of a population gains access to such modern goods and services, a marked decline in birth rates will result.

In most poor countries, a large proportion of the population traditionally seeks a high number of births per family. A major drop in fertility occurs only when this population group with high birth rates and relatively low socio-economic status shifts to reduced fertility levels. Thus, the target population that *must* be affected if a substantial decline in fertility is to occur is this same large majority of the population. Changes in the fertility behavior of the higher socio-economic status groups alone make very little difference, because these groups constitute only a minority of the population and a still smaller share of the nation's births. The challenge is therefore to create an environment in which the lower socio-economic groups will first choose to, and then easily be able to, limit family size. The need is not merely to expand the production of goods and services in a country, but also to distribute goods and services in a way that will markedly improve the well-being of the lower socio-economic groups.

This concept of a relationship between the distribution of socio-economic benefits and population growth has definite implications for development policies. Before considering either these implications or the limits of the hypothesis, however, it is important to take a closer look at those socio-economic variables that appear to affect decisions to limit family size.

COMPONENTS OF THE
DEVELOPMENT-FERTILITY CONTINUUM

The continuum of fertility decisions just described is affected by a complex set of social and economic factors. Knowledge of what these factors are and of the way in which they relate to decisions on family size is still rudimentary, and much additional research is badly needed. The complexity of interrelationships has made it difficult, if not impossible, to isolate direct causal links. The following discussion of key variables presents the most basic and consistent observations that could be drawn from the available information.

Education. Reduced fertility has often been related to the spread of education. Educational development, in the broad sense of the word, of course encompasses a wide variety of activities—ranging from an increase in schools and classroom activities, to use of more advanced farming or industrial technologies, or improvements in literacy skills developed outside of the classroom. In tested instances, all of these activities have appeared to be closely related to reduced fertility.

The data from the Cauquenes area in Chile presented in Table 2 indicate a continuum in the relationship between educational and fertility levels that appears to support the development-

TABLE 2

The Relationship between Educational Level
and Fertility in Cauquenes, Chile

Educational Level of Women Interviewed	Average Number of Births Per Couple	Per Cent of Population
No formal education	4.86	20.2
Some primary school	3.40	48.3
Complete primary school	1.26	13.1
Some secondary school	1.21	14.4
Complete secondary school	1.69	4.0

SOURCE: Carmen Miro and Walter Mertens, "Influences Affecting Fertility in Urban and Rural Latin America," *Milbank Memorial Fund Quarterly* 46, no. 3 (July 1968), p. 105.

fertility hypothesis. The site of the data—the wine-producing provincial city of Cauquenes and its environs—is a remote area in the coastal mountains that is among the poorest regions of Chile. The region's small, traditionally operated farms are dispersed over hilly terrain. The majority of the population in Cauquenes has little, if any, education and also has high average birth rates. Further declines in family size among the relatively advanced educational groups have little effect on population growth rates, because these small groups already demonstrate substantially reduced numbers of births per family. Eighty-seven per cent of the children in the village belong to the 68 per cent of the adult population that lacks a full primary education. Any major reduction in population growth can only result from changes affecting this group.

The following figure further illustrates the correlation between the educational achievements of parents and family size in a variety of social settings.

This Figure offers tempting support for a conclusion that primary education is an impressive starting point for fertility reduction. Further support is presented in Annex D, which shows a high correlation in Latin America between rising literacy levels and declining birth rates. As noted previously, however, observed correlations are a step removed from a reliable understanding of causal links.

Several explanations have been offered of why participation in education may lead to a desire for reduced family size. Education can affect the norms and values of persons in such a way that they begin to question traditional practices of their parents or other authority figures. It has been shown that persons who go to school or who are literate tend to be early adopters of innovations and also have a greater opportunity to come into contact with "change agents" such as health planners or family planning advisors.[9] Increased understanding of reproduction as well as improved access to family planning information link a more specific aspect of educational development to fertility reduction. Furthermore, there is usually also some correlation between extent of education

FIGURE 2
**Births per Woman by Educational Level
in Buenos Aires, Rio de Janeiro,
Hungary, and the United States**

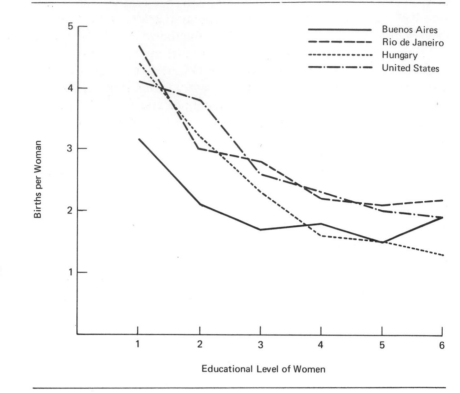

NOTE: Educational levels 1-6 shown in the graph stand for the following educational categories: 1 (No School), 2 (Some Primary), 3 (Complete Primary), 4 (Some Secondary), 5 (Complete Secondary), 6 (Higher Education). The grouping of the educational categories for Hungary and the United States has been slightly revised from the original presentation of the data. The South American data is for live births per woman. The Hungarian data is for births per married woman. The U.S. data is for white, married women aged 45 to 49.

SOURCES: Data for Buenos Aires and Rio de Janeiro from Carmen Miro and Walter Mertens, "Influences Affecting Fertility in Urban and Rural Latin America," *Milbank Memorial Fund Quarterly*, July 1968, p. 105. Data for Hungary from Jerzy Berent, "Causes of Fertility Decline in Eastern Europe and the Soviet Union," *Population Studies* 24 (1 and 2), 1970. Data for United States from U.S. Bureau of the Census, "Women by Number of Children Ever Born," Final Report PC(2)-3A, in *U.S. Census of Population: 1960, Subject Reports* (Washington, D.C.: GPO, 1964), p. 100.

and income level, and higher income generally brings with it other factors, such as improved health. Extended education is also likely to cause delay in marriage, as well as an increase in vocational alternatives to child-rearing. All of these explanations help to account for the particularly strong correlation observed between female education and family size.[10]

As extended education becomes available, the period during which a child is dependent on parental support increases. As a result, parents may have to decide whether to have two children and educate them fully, or whether to have six without being able to educate them. Interviews with Taiwanese farmers indicate that "those farmers who have high educational aspirations *and* know something about educational costs show a much higher incidence of contraceptive use and a smaller ideal family size than others."[11]

This series of explanations of how education or literacy affect fertility is far from exhaustive. Furthermore, it does not "prove" that efforts to increase educational standards provide a direct or efficient route to reduced family size. Since every government devotes some resources to education, however, questions concerning the effectiveness of educational strategies should be viewed in that context. Alternative education policies will be considered further in Chapter II.

Health. Some observers have gone so far as to blame improved health conditions for "causing" the population explosion. Health services accompanied by improvements in nutrition and sanitation certainly have helped to reduce death rates. It should be noted, however, that improved health care, along with other social and economic improvements, also ultimately contributes to birth rate reduction.

Health services offer a natural springboard for family planning and birth control programs. Persons who perceive a positive relationship between modern health care and well-being are most likely to adopt positive attitudes toward modern birth control techniques. Support for this thesis has been noted by Carl Taylor on the basis of two decades of health care and family planning experiments in India.[12]

A Harvard University team led by David Heer has emphasized how important the assurance of high rates of survival is for the motivation for smaller families.[13] Where mortality rates were very high, the Harvard study showed, parents generally had as many children as possible. Where death rates were low and life expectancy 50 years or more, however, reductions in the death rate led to reduction in the total population growth rate; when the survival of a son had been ensured by most families, the number of children born fell faster than the decrease in deaths among existing children. A related study found, moreover, that families in India would still need to bear an average of 6.3 children to be certain (at a 95 per cent level of probability) of the survival of one son. Indian fertility was observed to be entirely consistent with the family size necessary to ensure the survival of a son.[14]

As prospects for child survival improve, a shift also occurs along the demographic continuum. In the past, birth rates generally have not fallen significantly until child survival had improved for an extended period. In East Pakistan (now Bangladesh) women who experienced the loss of a child had 0.5 children more on the average than other mothers.[15] In Egypt, data on a sample of women aged 45-47 years showed that those who had lost a child had more births and desired a larger number of surviving children than those who had not lost a child.[16] These recent studies demonstrate the relationship between the frequently noted observation of a correlation between improved child survival and reduced fertility over extended periods on the basis of *aggregate* data, and the observation of a correlation between improved child survival and immediate changes in decisions to limit the number of children *at the family level.* These studies suggest that if fewer families experience the loss of a child, changes in aggregate fertility are soon likely to follow. More research is necessary, however, to satisfactorily explain this complex relationship.

Urbanization. Urban residence has been consistenly correlated with low fertility in most regions of the world. In Latin America, for instance, family size in rural areas and small towns has been shown to be almost twice that in large urban centers.[17] Other examples of this correlation can be drawn from the experience of countries as different from one another as Lebanon, India, Hungary, Japan, and the Soviet Union.[18]

Various theories have been offered to explain this relationship. Health and family planning facilities are generally more accessible in cities than in rural areas. The greater availability of schools—and the power of example—are more likely to make parents take their children out of productive activities in cities than in rural areas; the fact that children thus become economic liabilities rather than assets may lead families to limit births.

Living space is generally more limited in urban areas, and the crowding effect of an additional child is more likely to have an impact on the child-bearing decisions of urban parents. Employment opportunities for both men and women are more apt to be outside the home, creating a greater conflict between employment and child-bearing opportunities. Increased familiarity with the relatively modern sector of the economy may stimulate new savings patterns and consumption aspirations,[19] and, in turn, influence attitudes toward planning family size.

All of the above have been cited as factors in the correlation between urbanization and reduced family size. Some, such as crowding, are based on *problems* of urbanization and therefore offer no positive guidelines for rural development policies. Others do have useful general implications for development planning. For instance, the availability of education and health facilities is planned through government policy and *can* be extended to the countryside. Likewise, "non-traditional" employment activities and new savings patterns may be influenced by the introduction of new farming techniques, credit opportunities, or middle level industries in rural areas. In Ceylon, for example, where access to health and educational facilities is quite similar in rural and urban areas, there is only a marginal difference in birth rates between the two.[20]

Thus urbanization *per se* may not be as important to limiting family size as other indirect factors that result in increased access to modern goods and services. Fertility-level differences *among* urban areas offer a further indication of the relatively greater importance of socio-economic variables in affecting birth rates. The eight Latin American cities in which the Latin American Demographic Center (CELADE) in Santiago, Chile, collected data during the 1960s ranked as shown in Table 3 in terms of their fertility rates. These differences appear to be related to some extent to the general socio-economic and cultural context of the Latin American countries in which the particular cities are found. While they prove little in and of themselves, these correlations support the thesis that low rates of urban fertility reflect relatively high access to the modern socio-economic system.

TABLE 3

Number of Live Births for All Women Interviewed
(Standardized According to Buenos Aires Age Distribution)

Buenos Aires	1.49
Rio de Janeiro	2.48
Santiago	2.51
Panama	3.14
San Jose	3.28
Caracas	3.42
Bogota	3.64
Mexico City	3.79

SOURCE: Carmen Miro and Walter Mertens, "Influences Affecting Fertility in Urban and Rural Latin America," *Milbank Memorial Fund Quarterly* 46, no. 3 (July 1968), p. 96.

Mobility. Related to both urbanization and modernization, mobility—in both its social and geographical senses—is likely to affect fertility. Opportunities for social mobility, or the development of opportunities for social improvement, also can affect motivation for family planning. Aspirations toward educational opportunities—previously noted in the case of Taiwanese farmers[21]—seem to have a direct effect on fertility. Movement from villages to cities or from town to town, is likely to break some ties in extended families. In such a situation, young people may postpone marriage. If men leave their families often and for extended periods to work in other sections of the country, this, too, is likely to have some effect on the birth rate. Moreover, if parents cannot expect to live with their adult children, they are less likely to have children for the sake of support in old age.[22] Movement away from the traditional family home may itself stimulate other breaks from traditional patterns—such as adoption of family planning.

Income. In recent years, there has been considerable debate as to the role of income in influencing fertility decisions. Cross-national studies have indicated that as incomes rise, births decline. Figure 3 indicates the percentage of families who desire four or more children—at different income levels and in a cross-section of countries.

While remaining wary of oversimplified conclusions, it is interesting to note that average income levels of the poorest 60 per cent of the population correlate much more closely with fertility levels than do average incomes of the entire population. In a comparison of 40 less developed countries, an increase of $10 in the income of the lower 60 per cent was associated with a 0.7 per thousand decline in the crude birth rate, whereas a $10 increase in average income was associated with only a 0.3 per thousand de-

FIGURE 3

**Relationship Between Desired Family Size
and Income Levels in Selected Countries**

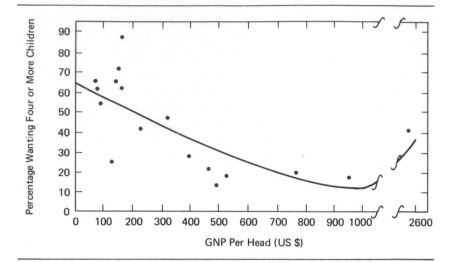

NOTE: The upward turn of the graph at the high income level (far right) is due to the fact that the desired family size in the United States, at the time the data was gathered several years ago, was substantially larger than in countries at intermediate levels of development. It has since declined sharply and is now in line with the long-term decline indicated by other countries.

SOURCE: Bernard Berelson, "KAP Studies on Fertility," in Berelson et al., eds., *Family Planning and Population Programs* (Chicago: University of Chicago Press, 1966), p. 663.

cline.[23] These data provide further support for the hypothesis that the factor most crucial to fertility is increased distribution of income (and services) to the large low-income portion of the population.[24] The nations or large regional areas that have begun the demographic transition at a relatively low total economic level have all done so simultaneously with a broad distribution of added income and increased well-being.[25]

Two basic points can be made about the relationship between income and fertility in the developing countries: 1) An increase in family income in and of itself is not as important as the changes in circumstances that it permits. These factors, such as better health or increased access to education, lead to reductions in family size. Income increases among the poor are likely to stimulate far more of these crucial secondary changes than comparable increases in the total income of the affluent. 2) It is not sufficient to cite trends in GNP without including additional information about how resources are distributed among the populace of any given country. If income gains are concentrated among only 5 per cent of the population, then broad reductions in fertility cannot be expected.

Employment. As the babies born in the 1950s have entered the labor market, unemployment has emerged as one of the most basic social and political problems in many poor countries. Employment is of course the key to access to income—which, in turn, opens the way to improved health, education, and nutrition. Reliable job opportunities of course also affect the security of the family. When only marginal employment is available—such as peddling in the cities, or harvest work in rural areas—then families may consider it necessary to have as many children as possible to contribute to family support. When parents are sure of holding jobs, however, they can afford to limit their family size and invest in the health and welfare of the children they have.

For women, the increased availability of employment outside the household tends to offer an alternative to child-bearing; women who work—particularly outside the house—are more likely to postpone marriage, postpone having children, or limit family size. Most studies completed thus far—throughout the developed countries as well as in urban areas of the developing countries— indicate that as women find employment opportunities outside of the home, family size declines. This correlation between female labor force participation and fertility is less apparent in village and rural areas of the developing countries, where employment is less likely to remove the woman from her household.[26] However, in Mauritius and in Barbados, high rates of female employment appear to have contributed to rapid birth declines.[27] Evidence of such a trend also was found in the United Arab Republic, where "female activity in the non-agricultural labor force is powerfully and directly associated with female education and inversely associated with . . . fertility."[28]

Expanding Opportunities for Development. The composite variable that may in fact have the greatest influence on the small family norm is the combination of factors that expand the individual's interests and sources of satisfaction beyond the traditional family. A couple living in poverty, without work and without social aspirations or hope of participation in the progress of the society, may find no experiences in life as important or enjoyable as child-bearing and child-rearing. Although the opportunity for improvement of individual or community welfare will not, in itself, change the desirability of having children, it may for the first time offer parents attractive alternatives to child raising. This may be what T. N. Carver had in mind when, in 1924, he defined the Standard of Living as "the number of desires that take precedence in the individual's choice over the effective desire for offspring."[29] Unfortunately, research efforts to verify Carver's concept are only beginning to attract the interest or support which may lead to a more scientific conclusion.[30]

Another way of looking at the question of expanded access to modern opportunities and its effect on fertility is to focus on quantitative data and to consider the experience of those countries where there have been significant fertility declines. James Kocher has observed that "comparative experience from many countries suggests that economic growth which is highly distorted and which fails to bring real benefits and more modern life styles to the large bulk of the population cannot be expected to be accompanied by sustained fertility decline." Where small farmers, as well as the wealthy, have been involved in modernization, reductions in family size have ensued. Since the majority of the population in the less developed countries will, in the foreseeable future, have rural occupations, those countries in which the small farmers have access to an improved living standard through modern farming techniques are the ones that are most likely to experience declines in the birth rate.[31]

While Kocher examined evidence only in those countries which had experienced national reductions in population growth, mounting evidence demonstrates that the process he described also applies, given similar conditions, to countries whose overall birth rate is not declining. Thus, in Mexico—a country in which most small farmers have benefited little from modern agricultural development—the birth rate for the entire population remains high. *Within* Mexico, however, those few small farmers who have adopted new farming techniques tend to have smaller families.[32]

James Hooker has summarized this process from a still different perspective. In discussing the plight of the Black population of Rhodesia, Hooker suggests that, *"given the chance*, most Africans would enter a home owners' scheme, tie themselves to the mortgage . . . fret over school fees, do all the things the middle classes do. The result would be fewer children."[33] It is probable that development efforts which do not create such opportunities will be slow to lead to reductions in births.

DIFFICULTIES IN RELATING DEVELOPMENT TO FERTILITY

A major and continuing problem faced by researchers working on the correlation of various indicators of development and fertility is the lack of data that adequately reflect the actual social and economic conditions of the societies concerned. Mortality and literacy rates give some indication of the number of persons actually benefiting from modern services, and these indicators, which reflect "distribution" most clearly, tend to correlate most closely with fertility patterns. Even this information, however, is often of questionable accuracy. In the most general sense, there is a great need for data that reflect the conditions of individual households and that are collected in a consistent fashion so that they can be used for comparative analysis. Although the lack of data makes precise measurement of causal links impossible, it does not strongly limit the applicability of the central hypothesis. We do know which general combination of factors results in reduced birth rates, and we certainly know which portion of the population must be affected if national fertility is to decline significantly.

Some questions have been raised about the development-fertility hypothesis on the ground that differences in fertility may result primarily from cultural or religious differences. The facts that 1) very high population growth rates continue in Latin America despite the region's relatively high per capita income, and that 2) the most successful examples of rapidly declining birth rates in countries with low per capita incomes are to be found in East Asia, have led many to argue that Catholicism is the dominant reason for the former and that Chinese cultural attributes are responsible for the latter.

Obviously, religious and cultural variables do affect attitudes toward family size, and far more research is needed in this area. But comparable policies and programs have been shown to have roughly comparable effects in *different* religious and cultural settings. Thus education correlated similarly with fertility in both Chile and Hungary. Farmers who adopt modern farming techniques and experience social and economic benefits as a result have smaller families in Mexico as well as in Taiwan or the Indian Punjab. Sweden, a non-Catholic, industrialized country, has the same low population growth rate (with its population doubling only every 88 years) as Italy, a Catholic, industrialized country. Morocco, Syria, Pakistan, Ecuador, Panama, and Paraguay are all poor countries having exactly the same high population growth rate (with their populations doubling every 21 years); yet the first three are Moslem and the last three, Catholic.[34] Annex D illustrates the rough correlation between the general well-being of the population and birth rates for the developing countries of the Western Hemisphere (see p. 72).

With regard to the alleged greater Chinese cultural willingness to shift toward smaller families, it bears noting that similar improvements in education, health, income, and jobs apparently have had roughly comparable effects on the Singhalese in Ceylon, Indians and Tamals in Singapore, Blacks in Barbados, and Punjabis in India, as on Chinese in East Asia. While there is need for much more research on the impact of cultural and religious factors on birth rates, it is now sufficiently clear that the improved availability of jobs, income, and social services significantly affects attitudes toward family size in virtually *all* societies.

A qualification of the development-fertility hypothesis must, however, be applied to the treatment of the prospect for persons at the very poorest end of the socio-economic spectrum. For conceptual purposes, it is useful to describe the population in a developing country in terms of three groups, with generally consistent socio-economic status and fertility behavior. The first group has benefited from the modern socio-economic system and generally has a low fertility level. The second group maintains itself at a subsistence level in a traditional society without major opportunities for improvement; this group maintains only minor limitations on fertility. The third group is made up of persons whose relative socio-economic condition has worsened significantly, leaving them below any acceptable subsistence level. Such people may exhibit the fertility behavior of group one, for related reasons. Both groups one and three have changed from the traditional life style—group one because opportunities for improvement exist, and group three because they are no longer able to subsist along traditional patterns. Studies of rural Thailand and Bangladesh have illustrated this phenomenon. In relatively crowded and depressed areas of these countries, the individuals most willing to accept family planning were the landless or those with the smallest land holdings, the fewest other possessions, and the least education.[35] In the mass vasectomy camp held in Uttar Pradesh in February of 1972, economic incentives added to the tendency of the most depressed socio-economic groups to undergo vasectomy.[36] Severe national economic depression, forced migration from one area of a country to another, critical urban housing shortages, or crop failures have also resulted in at least temporary reductions in birth.

Thus birth rates may drop as a result of negative, as well as positive, social or economic changes. The more basic conclusion, however, is that people react rationally to a change in circumstances: when it makes sense to have fewer children, they have fewer children.

effective development strategies: sharing progress to reduce fertility

Although it still is not possible at this time to specifically measure   21
the relationship between socio-economic development and the
motivation for smaller families that results in reduced fertility, the
evidence shows that some policies clearly have greater impact on
the birth rate than others. This chapter will focus on those development strategies which appear to bring about reductions in population growth by improving economic and social welfare.

SHORTCOMINGS OF TRADITIONAL APPROACHES TO DEVELOPMENT

There is today a great deal of dissatisfaction with the results of
economic development efforts in the poor countries. This is evident within the less developed countries themselves, the international development community, the American public, and certainly the U.S. Congress. Disappointment and disillusionment exist
not so much because the goals of the 1960s were not attained as
because the ambitious growth goals set at the beginning of the
decade no longer seem adequate.

The objectives of the first United Nations Development Decade were expressed almost entirely in economic growth terms. The
goal was to raise the economic growth rate from approximately 3
per cent per annum to 5 per cent, which was expected to result in
modest gains in per capita income. At the end of the decade,
however, it was evident that heavy concentration on the pursuit of
economic growth more often than not resulted in worsening the
distribution of income. The general pattern appeared to be one
whereby the poorest quarter of society suffered a decline in its
share of national income. Indeed, in some situations the economic
well-being of this group appears to have deteriorated even in abso-
lute terms over the previous decade.[1]

Thus, although Pakistan's economy, for example, grew at a
healthy rate throughout most of the 1960s, unemployment increased, real wages in the industrial sector declined by one-third,
and the per capita income disparity between East and West Pak-

istan nearly doubled. In 1968, when GNP growth was at its peak, the government collapsed under the strain of social and economic pressures.[2]

To many, Brazil is today a brilliant example of economic success. Despite the country's rapid economic growth, however, a large portion of the population has not benefited measurably from the impressive increase in production (see Annex D). The share of the national income received by the poorest 40 per cent of the population declined from 10 per cent in 1960 to an estimated 8 per cent in 1970, whereas the share of the richest 5 per cent grew from 29 to 38 per cent during the same period. Thus throughout a decade of dramatic progress, the rich did very well while the poorer half of the population benefited only marginally.[3]

In the Philippines, too, the distribution of income appears to have worsened in the last two decades,[4] and in India the real income of the poorest 10 per cent of the population (50 million people) appears to have declined during a decade in which the GNP increased by 50 per cent.[5] Examples of this kind are legion, and it is clear that economic growth does not necessarily lead to the reduction of poverty or malnutrition within the lowest economic groups.

Not unrelated to the income distribution problem is the spreading unemployment common to all but a few developing countries. Measuring unemployment against a 40-hour work standard, one researcher, Harry T. Oshima, has estimated that in Pakistan, Ceylon, Malaysia, the Philippines, Bangladesh, and probably also in Indonesia, 15 per cent or more of the labor force is now unemployed.[6] India, now faced with 100,000 new entrants into the job market each week, has no program to create additional employment on a comparable scale.[7] It is now clear that traditional approaches to development are not very effective in coping with this problem. A rapid rate of economic growth may be necessary for other reasons, but it is not by itself sufficient to reduce unemployment. In the case of Latin America, for example, it is estimated that there must be an average rate of economic growth of 8 per cent during the 1970s if the region is to even hold the line on unemployment.[8]

Unfortunately, Western economic experience does not have much to offer toward a solution of this dilemma. The rate of population growth in the poor countries is, on the average, more than twice as high as any previous extended population increase in the West. Furthermore, in the West, vast areas of uncultivated land were open to expanding population—a situation that very few poor nations face in the coming decades. As a result, not only is the dependent population in the current developing countries (those persons unable to support themselves) much larger in percentage terms, but the demand for employment is also growing at unprecedented rates.

The failure of traditional development models in the poor countries is in part the result of the rapid growth of population itself. There is another side to this coin, however, in that these development models have failed to slow population growth. For the most part, only a small elite has started to practice fertility control in those developing countries which have followed a tradi tional approach to development. This small elite is generally the same group that is benefiting from the modern social and economic system.

In terms of the development-fertility hypothesis outlined in the previous chapter, traditional development models have led only a small portion of the total population to a socio-economic level conducive to family planning. The remainder of the society, still living at a subsistence level, continues to support the relatively high average number of births. What is needed is a development strategy that will distribute the benefits of progress more evenly.

NEW APPROACHES TO DEVELOPMENT

The spreading awareness that traditional development models have failed has led to reexamination of development strategies. Recent innovations by several development theorists represent a significant departure from the standard approach with its central focus on economic growth.

Mahbub ul Haq, a principal architect of Pakistan's development program in the early 1960s who is acutely aware of that program's shortcomings, argues that:

23

> development goals must be defined in terms of progressive reduction and eventual elimination of malnutrition, disease, illiteracy, squalor, unemployment and inequalities. We were taught to take care of our GNP as this will take care of poverty. Let us reverse this and take care of poverty as this will take care of the GNP. In other words, let us worry about the *content* of GNP even more than its rate of increase.[9]

Mr. Haq has now examined the Chinese experience as a substantive example of one alternative development model. From 1950 to 1970, the rate of economic growth in China probably was not above 4 per cent annually, but there appeared to have been major improvements in access to health care and educational services over the same period. Underemployment seems to be better controlled in China than, for example, in India or Pakistan, and the distribution of goods and services also appears to be more equitable. As more information becomes available about China, we should be able to learn from both its successes and its failures.

In another effort to "rethink development," Robert Shaw has concluded that "the way to tackle the employment problem is to work for a better balance between rural and urban areas, between various sectors of the economy, between the use of scarce capital and abundant labor, and between the rich and the poor."[10] Such efforts not only improve living conditions, but also increase efficiency, since the vast underutilized labor reserves in the developing countries also appear to have a high productive potential.[11]

The lack of hard data in this area is indicative of the low level of priority that has been given such suggestions in the past. Economists often refer in a disturbingly casual fashion to "unemployment of *about* 10 or 20 per cent."[12] Malnutrition "appears" to be increasing in many poor countries, and distribution patterns "seem" to be growing worse over time. Data which clearly depict distribution patterns within countries have seldom been collected, as many economists long assumed that "distribution will take care of itself" once production is increased sufficiently.[13] New attitudes need to be reflected in new research priorities.

INCOME DISTRIBUTION

Given the concept of a development-fertility continuum, the key is to distribute benefits of development so that a large majority, rather than a small elite, will reach a socio-economic level conducive to reduced fertility at an early stage. This pragmatic approach to the population threat is complementary to ethical demands for "social justice." It rests on the need to select those strategies and those technologies which are "appropriate" for the specific problems of different less developed countries.

Clearly, it is the change in reaching a broader group with more goods and services—not simply a rising per capita GNP—that has the most significant effect on the motivation for smaller families and, thereby, on fertility rates. This is very evident if, for example, one compares the experiences of Taiwan and the Philippines in terms of 1) their present distributions of income and changes in income distribution over time, and 2) their fertility rates.

In the years represented in Figure 4, the per capita income in Taiwan was approximately $246, or similar to that of the Philippines, which was $235. There was, however, a considerable discrepancy between the distributions of income in the two countries. The highest 10 per cent of the population in the Philippines was significantly wealthier than the same group in Taiwan, but the lowest 20 per cent was more than twice as well off in Taiwan. Moreover, there also is evidence that in Taiwan, income distribution has improved markedly over time, whereas in the Philippines it has become more and more concentrated among the wealthiest 20 per cent of the population.[14] These two factors help to explain why a much greater share of the population appears to have reached the socio-economic level conducive to reduced fertility in Taiwan than in the Philippines.[15] Comparisons similar to that between Taiwan and the Philippines can also be made between Barbados, Argentina, South Korea, Singapore, Uruguay, Cuba, Costa Rica, or China on the one hand, and Venezuela, Mexico, Brazil, and many of the other Latin American countries on the other.

The distribution of the benefits of progress is very much influenced by the development strategy followed in each sector. It is possible to design a health care system that will benefit only the urban elite, or one that will benefit the entire population. The same is true of education or transportation. The following pages focus on alternative development strategies for key sectors of the economy.

AN OPTIMAL HEALTH CARE SYSTEM

The basic problem in delivering health care is, of course, to determine how to improve the health of as much of the population as possible with limited resources. Alternative strategies result in varying levels of training and support of physicians, nurses, midwives, and other paramedical workers and pharmacists, as well as

FIGURE 4

**Distribution of Income in Taiwan
and the Philippines, by Income Groups**

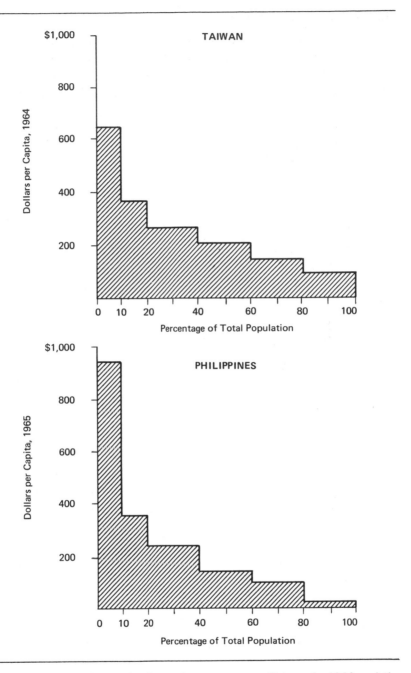

NOTE: The figures in these charts represent Taiwan in 1964 and the Philippines in 1965.

SOURCE: David Turnham, "Income Distribution: Measurement and Problems," in Andrew E. Rice, ed., *International Development 1971, Development Targets for the 1970's: Jobs and Justice* (Dobbs Ferry, N. Y.: Oceana Publications, 1972), p. 40.

in varying levels of capital investment in hospitals, clinics, mobile health units, and other facilities. The usual approach thus far has been to focus on training highly skilled medical doctors and building hospitals—two central components of the Western health system. The effect of this approach in countries where financial resources are scarce has been to provide relatively high-quality health care for a small urban elite, while depriving most of the population of health services altogether. A recent Agency for International Development study of health care noted that:

> AID's 40-some client governments are spending about $15 billion annually on health services. This expenditure has little effect on the lives of most people. Service delivery systems reach 10 per cent of the people or less. The copying of the developed country health apparatus has been expensive and inappropriate, and has had comparatively little to do with reductions in mortality or ill health in the LDCs.[16]

Experience in several countries illustrates more appropriate strategies. Ceylon, for instance, has made a concerted effort over the past two decades to improve health facilities by training large numbers of paramedical workers while maintaining a relatively small core of fully trained doctors. Thus, although the ratio of physicians to population has not changed greatly over the two decades—in 1967 there was still only one physician per 4,060 people—life expectancy has increased from 54 to 62 years over the same period. These results provide a marked contrast to the situation in Turkey, where—with a similar per capita governmental expenditure for health care, and despite Turkey's much higher per capita GNP—decidedly inferior health services were offered to the vast majority of the population. The Turkish health system has concentrated on the needs of urban areas, using conventional means, although many rural areas in the country do not even have one physician per 10,000 persons. AID descriptions of the situation in the two countries find Ceylon making "tremendous progress in improving health conditions," while health facilities in Turkey are "barely adequate to meet minimum needs."[17]

A comparison of the health care delivery systems of Turkey and South Korea further underlines weaknesses in the type of approach taken by Turkey. While the number of doctors, dentists, and midwives per thousand people in the two countries is roughly the same, the number of pharmacists per thousand is more than five times greater in South Korea than in Turkey and the number of nurses twice as great.[18] Access to health services in rural areas is far superior in the case of Korea.

The pronounced edge in low-cost medical treatment gives Korea and Ceylon a life expectancy about 4 years and 8 years longer, respectively, than that in Turkey, and an infant mortality rate of 53 and 50 per thousand compared to 119 per thousand in Turkey.

Perhaps the most dramatic improvements in health care in the last two decades have occurred in China. Inheriting a seriously inadequate health care system, the government placed high priority on improvements in this field. Initial steps were taken to improve environmental sanitation and personal hygiene. Major pests were exterminated, and millions of persons were vaccinated. During the mid-1960s, doctors were sent out to rural areas, and mobile medical teams were assigned to service remote areas of the country. Major emphasis was placed on paramedical education, as well as on short-term medical training courses for both full time and part-time medical and public health workers. In many cases people were recruited from the countryside, trained in nearby medical centers, and then returned to their villages. Most recently, China has instituted a system of "barefoot doctors" trained to provide first-aid, give innoculations, and carry out simple health procedures—including the performance of abortions and the distribution of contraceptives. Cases that are too complicated for these "barefoot doctors" are referred to fully trained doctors, who have been allocated throughout China. As more information about China becomes available, it will be possible to assess these programs more carefully.[19]

The provisions of hospital services can be evaluated in terms similar to those applied to medical personnel. In many cases, governments have devoted a large portion of their total investment in health services to the construction of a few modern hospitals in urban areas, while the needs of rural communities were wholly ignored. A new hospital may be accessible to only a small and relatively privileged portion of the population; a similar level of investment in rural clinics and dispensaries might reach far more people. Until a minimal base of medical aid is available to a large majority of the population, the "benefits" of hospital construction should perhaps be calculated in terms of lives lost due to failure in the distribution of health services.

The importance of at least rudimentary health delivery systems assumes yet another dimension when it is recognized that such services affect general well-being, child survival, and the extension of family planning, and therefore play an important role in attaining the socio-economic environment in which parents will choose to limit their family size.

AN APPROPRIATE EDUCATION POLICY

Educational strategies have received growing attention recently from both researchers and policy-makers, but sharp differences of opinion continue as to the best policy approaches. Problems that have arisen reinforce the need for new ideas in the field—for new strategies that break away from traditional Western patterns.

A universal educational system can quickly absorb the financial and administrative talents of any government. But a system that opens educational opportunities to only a small minority of the population can rapidly institutionalize a strongly hierarchical social relationship. A further dilemma is that if efforts are made to spread high levels of education widely—under tremendous economic constraints and according to the Western model—the quality of education is likely to become so diluted and so irrelevant to the society's need for skills that the entire effort can become socially disruptive. Thus governments waste money to provide "formal degrees" that may be meaningless in terms of skills or knowledge. In many poor countries, those who have attained a high level of education find that no appropriate jobs are available to them. Those with sophisticated medical or scientific training often migrate to Europe or the United States (where there are now some 30,000 doctors from developing countries) in response to lucrative job offers. At the same time, often because of the wrong educational priorities, the majority of the population remains de-

27

prived of even elementary levels of education. This clearly results in rising frustration among those who are educated as well as among those who continue to lack minimum educational skills.

It may be useful to recall in this context our earlier discussion of the relationship observed between female education and fertility. In the examples drawn from rural Chile, Rio de Janeiro, Buenos Aires, and Hungary (see Figure 2, p. 12), the most striking contrast was that between women with no education at all and those with a primary or elementary school education. Women who had completed primary school averaged about two children fewer than those who had not. Carmen Miro and Walter Mertens have observed that:

> the sharp decline in fertility [among those educated] at the primary school level may have some important implications for those considering population policies in Latin America. In the event that this decline could be considered general over Latin America, universality of complete elementary education or its equivalent could bring some important changes in the level of fertility.[20]

28   It is frequently asserted that at a certain level of educational experience, generally identified empirically with completed elementary-level training, individuals begin to question traditional family patterns, and become more open to alternative life styles and new practices—perhaps including modern family planning.

National educational strategies at present vary widely in terms of the portion of the population they are designed to reach. This is illustrated by differences between countries in the distribution of expenditures by level of education. The disbursal of public funds in South Korea, for example, makes the education system in that country accessible to a much wider segment of the total population than is the case in Brazil. According to government sources in both countries, in 1970, two-thirds of the Korean population between the ages of 5 and 14 was in primary school, while only one-half of the same group was in school in Brazil. In general, strategies focusing on widespread primary education are likely to affect fertility more than those strategies which emphasize higher education for a smaller segment of the population.

In Tanzania, for example, President Julius Nyerere has stressed the need to develop new models for education. Conscious of problems of unemployment and the need to develop labor-intensive activities in rural areas, he has helped build rural training centers. By giving an agricultural bias to education, he hopes to encourage both a scientific outlook and the willingness to apply it to work on the farm.[21] The problem faced by President Nyerere and other leaders is that of creating educational opportunities that will allow for mass participation and maximum efficiency, and that will provide the type of education that is most useful for those receiving it.

Recently a great deal of interest has been generated by attempts to integrate 1) "formal education," characterized by the "familiar hierarchical educational structure," and 2) "nonformal education," or "any organized program of learning carried on out-

FIGURE 5

**Allocation of Government Funds According to Level
of Education in South Korea and Brazil**

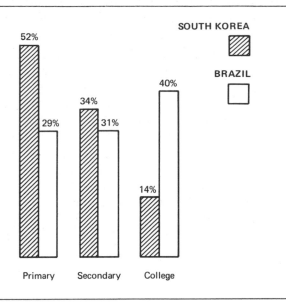

SOURCES: *Publicación Anuario Brasileiro de Educaçao, 1964*, pub-
lished by Brazil's Ministry of Education and Culture, 1966, p. 29; and *Social
Development, 1970*, published by South Korean Ministry of Health and
Social Affairs, 1970, p. 233.

side the framework."[22] In successful efforts to provide nonformal
education in the Comilla district of Bangladesh and in Taiwan it
has been observed that:

> where there has not yet been much development, low-level,
> nonformal training, carried out in the context of modernizing
> situations, is one of the keys to getting people involved in de-
> velopment, and a way for people gradually to move out of
> the low productivity knowledge base of the lore of nature and
> into the high productivity knowledge base of modern
> science.[23]

The precise effect of such educational involvement on family size
is still not clear, and this is one of many areas where additional
research is badly needed. If, however, such education resulted in
increased willingness to innovate, increased exposure to modern
contraceptive information, and increased access to the modern
socio-economic system, as well as in postponement of marriage
and child-bearing, then reductions in births would follow.

A MAJOR AGRICULTURAL
DEVELOPMENT EFFORT

Rural development efforts around the world reflect a wide range
of decisions regarding the selection of the technologies, land own-
ership policies, terms of credit, and other measures that are the
most likely to have a great impact on development.

Perhaps the most dynamic force in current rural development
is the "green revolution"—the introduction of new seed varieties

and farming techniques which offer vast improvements in crop yields. For some, the new seeds have brought a measure of hope in an otherwise hopeless situation, while for others the same developments threaten to result in unemployment and greater poverty. In 1971, for example, India achieved self-sufficiency in cereals for the first time in recent decades; in that year, its farmers produced all the cereals that the market would absorb at prevailing prices. At the same time, however, malnutrition among at least some segments of the rural poor appears to have increased.[24] At least part of this problem can be attributed to very uneven land distribution patterns and to the related problem of a growing force of landless laborers, who now number more than 60 million.

Realizing the genetic potential of the new seeds requires intensive farming, involving increased use of water, fertilizer, and energy. The great risk is that those farmers who double their yields per acre with the new wheats and rices will wish to convert their profits—after tripling and quadrupling production—into large tractors and grain combine harvesters. Although large-scale mechanization would have only a very modest effect on reducing production costs, it might displace enormous numbers of rural workers, adding them to the ranks of the unemployed.

Monetary policies that support the wealthy farmer's desire for mechanization by subsidizing import costs of large tractors or other machinery further aggravate this problem. As Lester R. Brown has noted, "the large farmer's penchant for mechanization can involve a frightful social cost. The danger inherent in the Green Revolution stems from that threat; the hope stems from the real economies and production increase that now can be realized on small farms with labor-intensive cultivation."[25]

Where unemployment and underemployment are rampant, as in Mexico, a strategy combining extensive land tenure reform, credit, marketing, and other services with the introduction of new crops can both provide more jobs and expand production. Owners of small farms and landless laborers who were formerly underemployed can—if seed, fertilizer, and tube wells or their equivalent for irrigation are made available—carry on intensive production on relatively small plots of land. Such reform permits unemployed and underemployed labor to be productively utilized—thus both expanding the national product and improving the distribution of income, by making certain that those at the relatively low end of the pay scale will be the ones to benefit most.

One vivid example of the successful implementation of this strategy is provided by Taiwan, where experimentation with improved crops, irrigation, and fertilizer began several years before the current interest in the new high-yielding seeds. Strict limits of 7.5 acres were placed on individual landholders, so that the average farm now consists of only 2.2 acres. An extensive system of farm cooperatives provides credit, markets, and new technology. As a result, those with small farms have been able to take advantage of the new crops; they have almost doubled their output in the past twenty years and have at the same time continued to provide employment for the rural population. The highly successful experience of Japan, where average farm size after land reform was 2.5 acres, also documents the potential benefits of broadly distributing land among those working on it.

FIGURE 6

Small Farm Efficiency in India, Taiwan, and Brazil

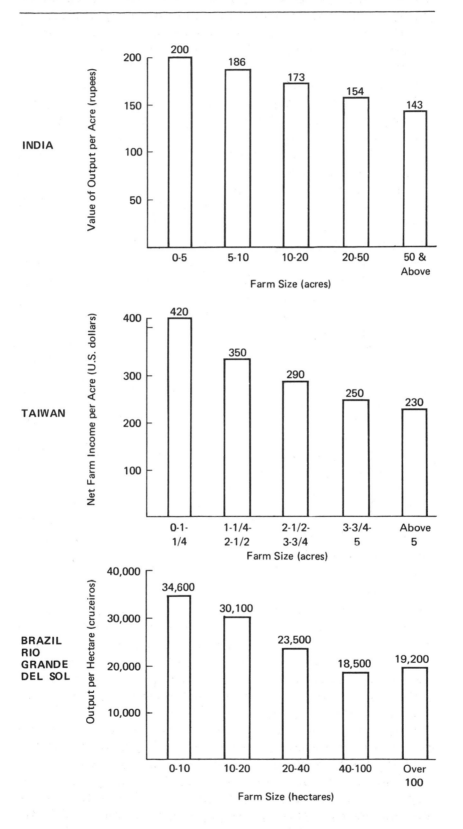

SOURCE: Edgar Owens and Robert Shaw, *Development Reconsidered* (Lexington, Mass.: D.C. Heath and Co., 1972), p. 60.

Data collected in several countries show that smaller farms, using relatively more labor and less capital, achieve greater output per acre than the larger farms. For example, farm output per acre in both India and Brazil is one-half to two-thirds higher on the smaller, more labor-intensive farms than on the larger, more mechanized ones. Within Taiwan, net farm income per acre on farms of less than 1.25 acres is nearly twice that realized on farms exceeding 5 acres.

THE NEED TO REDUCE JOBLESSNESS

The alternative agricultural development strategies discussed in the previous section illustrate some of the choices in technologies that affect employment levels during the development process. The methods of calculating efficiency used in industrially advanced societies, which have an abundance of capital and a scarcity of labor, have little relevance for the developing countries, where the relative values of labor and capital are different. As a result, strategies suited to the environment of the industrialized countries are often inappropriate for the developing countries. All too often, government monetary policies in developing countries, through unnecessarily low interest rates on industrial or agricultural loans and unrealistic exchange rates with foreign currencies, result in underpricing capital for machinery relative to labor, with the result that scarce capital is used to displace abundant labor. The price of labor and capital within a country must reflect the economic conditions of that country if they are to be employed in optimum combination with each other.

Examples from the rubber products industries of several developing countries clearly illustrate the employment implications of the selection of several alternative strategies. In the manufacture of rubber products, the amount of fixed capital required per laborer in several Asian countries varies as follows:[26]

Philippines	$2,645
Japan	1,756
India	1,272
Taiwan	756
South Korea	626

Thus in the Philippines and India, governmental policies resulted in far less employment for a given amount of investment than in Taiwan or South Korea. Experiences in road, bridge, and dam construction in China and a few other developing countries further illustrate the differing impact of technological alternatives. The basic message is that countries in which capital resources are scarce and labor is abundant must adopt policies which favor the use of the plentiful resource, labor, and do not subsidize use of scarce capital while widespread unemployment exists. Such a strategy is not only consistent with laws of comparative advantage, but also eases employment problems and aids in the distribution of wealth to a larger share of the total population.

Another form of labor-intensive production in the poor countries is found in relatively small-scale industrial activities. Several countries in East Asia have based their economies on such industries. Some nine tenths of Taiwan's "industries," for example, are

TABLE 4

Investment Cost of Increasing Production
and Labor's Share of Income,
by Factory Size, Taiwan, 1961

Size of Industry by Amount of Investment	Investment Cost of Increasing Output by $1.00	Labor's Share of Income per $1.00
Less than $2500	$1.97	$0.74
$2500 to $25,000	2.52	0.72
$25,000 to $250,000	3.26	0.50
$250,000 to $2.5 million	3.66	0.39
More than $25 million	4.46	0.31

SOURCE: S. C. Hsieh and T. H. Lee, *Agricultural Development and Its Contributions to Economic Growth in Taiwan* (Taipei: Joint Commission on Rural Reconstruction, 1966), p. 97. Cited in Edgar Owens and Robert Shaw, *Development Reconsidered* (Lexington, Mass.: D.C. Heath and Co., 1972), p. 116.

more aptly described as shops, since they employ 10 or fewer workers. They tend to employ a great deal of manpower and use rather few machines. Table 4 shows that the capital cost of increasing production in these small-scale industries is lower than that in the city-oriented factories. Furthermore, the high proportion of costs paid out in wages in labor-intensive industries stimulates local consumer demand.

Employment in the developing countries can be expanded not only by appropriate pricing policies, but also by strategies which change the composition of the demand for products of the industrial sector. Production of the luxury goods bought only by the wealthy in poor countries is generally capital-intensive rather than labor-intensive, whereas the goods poor people buy tend to require more local labor than capital. For example, producing an automobile in a developing country requires large amounts of capital but relatively little labor, whereas the production of bicycles, shirts, or food depends much more on use of local labor. Luxury products also generally require more foreign exchange reserves — either because the goods themselves are imported or because their manufacture demands more complex, capital-intensive machinery, which usually must be imported. Therefore it would seem that the poor countries would have much to gain by stimulating demand for those goods which are appropriate for local markets and require labor-intensive production techniques.[27] Most important in such an effort is the introduction of complementary policies to improve the welfare of the relatively poor and thereby increase the demand for such products.

THE POOR CAN SAVE

When the vast majority of a population is poor, the experiences and actions of this majority can have great impact on the success or failure of development efforts as a whole.

A persistent myth pervading development economics is that only the rich can save. This myth is commonly accepted both by Western economists who have studied savings and income ratios in the current Western setting, and by many tradition-bound government leaders who simply do not believe that the poor can save.

It is true that, given a fixed income, the poor have lower average savings rates than the rich. The same observation has been made in countries as diverse as India and the United States, and it is this fact among others that has led economists to assume that development plans must be based on the savings and investment potential of the rich alone. However, the lesson to be learned from examples such as those offered by the experiences of Taiwan, Singapore, and Uganda is that programs that provide access to credit and opportunities to develop resources can foster a highly responsible savings potential among the poor—who, because of their number, can greatly change the savings rates of their countries.

The government of Singapore's unique set of policies to encourage high rates of saving among low-income groups in the urban setting also deserves special mention. All workers—household, service, and industrial—contribute 12 per cent of their salaries, matched by their employers, to a National Provident Fund. Workers generally are enthusiastic about this high rate of withholding, because it can be used to cover the downpayments for their flats and to finance mortgage installments. Thus the benefits of these savings are not deferred until some remote retirement date. Largely through self-financing devices such as this, 80 per cent of Singapore's slum dwellers have had their living conditions dramatically improved in the last ten years.[28]

To take an example from another part of the world, between 1965 and 1969, there was a fourfold increase in personal savings in the Ankole District of Uganda. Moreover, during the same five-year period, members of the 77 village societies that make up the district union voted to forgo dividend payments of $78,000 in order to build capital.[29] Similar examples of small farmers' cooperatives that have stimulated high savings rates can be drawn from such diverse locations as Ceylon, the United Arab Republic, Colombia, Taiwan, or Korea.

Furthermore, when low-income groups have access to credit and own or rent their own homes or land, they are likely to save a major portion—in some cases as much as 20 or 30 per cent—of their income.[30] During the 1960s, savings among those with small farms in the Comilla District of Bangladesh rose to over $140,000 per year, and the gross assets of the District Federation, which consists of 301 village agricultural societies and 77 non-agricultural societies, are now $5 million.[31]

In many countries, only the rich have access to credit. As a result, the poor are excluded from the development process, and gaps between rich and poor widen. When the poor are enabled to save, and thus to participate in the modern sector of the economy, demand for the labor-intensive products in which they invest rises. Furthermore, when institutions are created to encourage and enable the poor to save, the demand for other services, such as better food, health care, and education systems is also likely to rise. In virtually every case where patterns of this type have been observed, reductions in birth rates have followed.

CUMULATIVE EFFECT OF APPROPRIATE DEVELOPMENT POLICIES ON THE BIRTH RATE

The question of distribution can be applied to almost every socio-economic variable. A country that distributes goods and services on an equitable basis can bring about improvements in the welfare of the relatively poor on a wide scale even if its total resource availability is low.

In Taiwan, for example, where income distribution is relatively equitable, health services have been extended throughout rural areas, and effective primary education is accessible to virtually all of the population. In Mexico, however, although average income is almost double that in Taiwan, the distribution of benefits is very limited, other social services also appear to be poorly shared, and the total welfare of the poorest groups is extremely low. As a result, the income of the poorest 20 per cent of the population is higher in Taiwan than in Mexico, and the "real income"—which includes measures for health and education—is noticeably higher in Taiwan.

Keeping in mind these differences in the distribution of income and services in the two countries, it is interesting to note that in Taiwan the birth rate dropped from 46 per thousand in 1952 to 31 per thousand in 1963, at which time a vigorous family planning program was introduced. The birth rate continued to fall thereafter, reaching 26 per thousand in 1970. In Mexico, on the other hand, the birth rate only declined from 44 per thousand to 42 per thousand over the eighteen-year period between 1952 and 1970. While the birth rate is declining in a few areas showing the greatest progress, this trend has not yet affected the majority of the Mexican population.

The contrast in living conditions between South Korea and Brazil further illustrates the relationship between alternative development strategies and birth rates.[32] In Korea, as a result of socio-economic improvements, the birth rate dropped from 45 per thousand in 1958 to 38 per thousand in 1964, by which time a family planning program had been implemented. The birth rate fell even faster thereafter, to about 30 per thousand in 1971—which reduced the population growth rate to approximately 2 per cent. In Brazil, on the other hand, the birth rate only declined from about 42 per thousand to 38 per thousand between 1958 and 1971; as in Mexico, this trend has not affected the majority of the population. Highly uneven distribution of income and of social services, as well as religious constraints and a lack of government support for family planning programs, have all contributed to the maintenance of Brazil's high population growth rate.

Although the available data are still incomplete, contrasts between the strategies adopted and actual results obtained in different Latin American countries appear to provide further supporting evidence for the development-fertility hypothesis (see Annex D). For instance, Uruguay, Chile, and Mexico (all Catholic countries) have comparable levels of GNP per capita, yet in 1970

TABLE 5

Comparison of Living Conditions
in South Korea and Brazil,
Selected Indicators

		South Korea	Brazil
Population Growth Rates	1958	3%	3%
	1964	2.7%	2.9%
	1971	2%	2.8%
Income per capita (1971)		$280	$395
GNP growth rates in the 1960s		9%	6%
Ratio of income, richest 20% to poorest 20% (1970)		5 to 1	25 to 1
Literacy (1970)		71%	61%
Infant deaths per 1,000 births (1970)		41	94
Unemployment		negligible	serious
Effective land reform		Yes	No
Family planning program		Yes	No

Uruguay had a birth rate of 22 per thousand; Chile, 28 per thousand; and Mexico, about 42 per thousand. Of these countries, Uruguay—which has no major family planning program—certainly has the longest history of "welfare economics," with extensive unemployment compensation as well as relatively successful health and education programs. Although Uruguay's economy has stagnated in recent years, a large portion of the population has attained relative financial security. Chile appears to fall in a middle category in these respects, while Mexico has the least equitable distribution of goods and services. Cuba, with less than half of Mexico's per capita GNP, but with an apparently far better distribution of goods and services to the poorest half of the population, has a birth rate of only 29 per thousand. Data on Argentina and Venezuela also support the hypothesis. Both countries have per capita incomes of about $1,000, the highest in Latin America. But Argentina, with a very good distribution of income and services, has a birth rate of 21 per thousand, while Venezuela, with close to, if not the worst, distribution of income in Latin America, still had a high birth rate of 41 per thousand in 1970. This difference in birth rates exists even though, as of 1971, the cumulative total of family planning acceptors was far higher in Venezuela than in Argentina.

The right mix in development policies can lead to reductions in births in most cultural settings. Thus in numerous cases—including Taiwan, South Korea, Ceylon, Barbados, Mauritius, Hong Kong, the Indian Punjab, Singapore, parts of Egypt, Costa Rica, Uruguay, and China—birth rates have begun to drop at a relatively early stage of development. In all of these cases, the reduction in births appears to have begun prior to the introduction of major family planning programs and seems to correlate with rather broad-based socio-economic improvements.

The effect on fertility of any single policy measure may not by itself be of great significance—just as no single change in a community is likely to cause many parents to further limit their family size. But development policies that focus on participation and increased access to benefits for the population as a whole do seem to produce a major impact on family size. In countries which have a relatively equitable distribution of health and education services, and which provide land, credit, and other income opportunities, the cumulative effect of such policies seems to be that the poorest half of the population is vastly better off than it is in countries with equal or higher levels of per capita GNP but poor distribution patterns. The combined effect of such policies has made it possible for some countries to reduce birth rates despite their relatively low levels of national production.

other policies that encourage
smaller families

A number of factors related to law and public policy, political and 39
social institutions, or changes in the social structure, may also
affect fertility regardless of the development strategy that is applied in any given country. Changes in these factors affect decisions on child-bearing and can cause either an increase or a decrease in desired family size. Such policies may, in effect, cause
changes in the motivation to limit family size without bringing
about substantial changes in the socio-economic continuum.

GOVERNMENT POLICIES TOWARD FAMILY SIZE

Every government reacts either directly or indirectly to questions
of family size and fertility. Until the last decade, most government
action directed specifically at population growth was designed to
increase family size. In recent years, however, many governments
have reversed their position—although the majority maintain "official" neutrality, and a few remain staunchly in favor of population
expansion.

    As of June 1971, twenty-four developing countries main-
tained official policies favoring family planning activities and gave
support to such programs; twenty-three supported family planning
activities but had no official policy; and fifty-five gave little or no
support to family planning activities and had no official policy.
Most of the large and most crowded developing countries were
among the twenty-four with official policy support for family
planning. Thus 96 per cent of the population of East Asia, 86 per
cent in the rest of Asia, 41 per cent in Africa, and 4 per cent in
Latin America live in countries with such official policies.[1] These
population policies certainly add a new, and in some cases hopeful
dynamic to the process of demographic change.

    Beyond the level of "official policy," there is great variety in
possible government positions on this question. Luke T. Lee and
his associates at Tufts University have noted that, despite claims
that the free decision to practice family planning is a basic human
right, systematic legal reforms to bring existing laws into line with

that recognition have seldom followed. They point out that:

> restrictions continue to hamper the importation, manufacture, advertisement, and transportation of contraceptives; the minimum age required for marriage remains low; education laws continue to forbid the teaching of family planning or sex education in schools; public health services remain unresponsive to the need for birth control counsel or clinics; the social welfare or income tax system may favor large families; and abortion codes contribute to high cost, high-risk, illegal operations.[2]

Changes in any policies of this sort may have some, as yet unmeasured, effect on fertility.

In many countries, rates of taxation are related to family size; changes in taxation policy can be expected—and in some cases have even been designed—to have an impact on decisions to limit or increase family size. The policies most familiar to Americans are those which allow tax deductions for each additional dependent. Such a policy establishes the right of each individual to a certain minimum level of resources, while it also lowers the cost of children and may, in some instances, act as an inducement for larger families. In the poor countries, however, most families do not earn taxable incomes in the first place, and governments must resort to approaches other than taxation to influence family size.

In Singapore, a crowded island community, the government has eliminated many of the more traditional incentives for having a large family. It has acted to change policies with regard to public housing by offering no additional subsidy to families with over three children. Mr. Lee Kuan Yew, Singapore's Prime Minister, adds that, eventually, "we may have to put disincentives or penalties on the other social services. Beyond three children, the costs of subsidized housing, socialized medicine, and free education should be transferred to the parent."[3]

Brazil, desiring to populate its inland areas, has assumed the opposite attitude toward population growth. National policy encourages births, and government officials propound the traditional argument linking national security to population size. The Ministry of Labor gives a supplement to families with more than six children; and the federal and state governments, as well as the National Social Security Institute, give employees bonuses for each new birth. Abortion and the advertising of contraceptives are illegal. Despite the official line, however, the attitude of the population itself has changed dramatically in the last four or five years. Consequently, the government is in a different position than it was in 1967, when it conducted a major campaign against contraception. The practice of family planning is spreading, especially in urban areas, and laws against abortion are not enforced. Major interest groups have expressed concern over the country's demographic problems, and high government officials "are known to favor a franker debate on the question, even though they remain silent for the moment."[4]

ABORTION POLICY

Wide variations exist in abortion laws and in the manner in which they are enforced. Romania, although not considered a "developing" country in global terms, nevertheless provides an example of how changes in government policy on abortion can affect the birth rate.

FIGURE 7

Annual Births per 1,000 Population (with monthly estimates) in Romania, 1966-1970

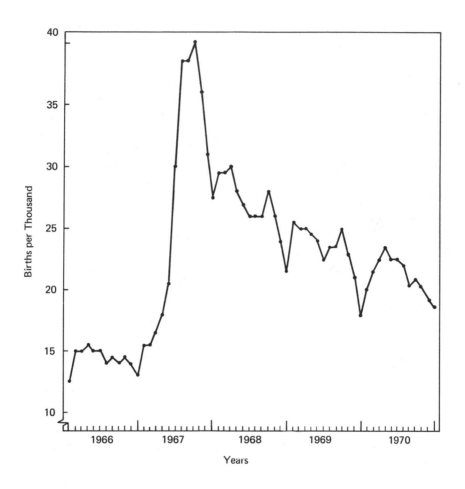

SOURCE: Henry P. David and Nicholas H. Wright, "Abortion Legislation: The Romanian Experience," *Studies in Family Planning* 2, no. 10 (October 1971), p. 207. Reprinted with permission of The Population Council.

After liberalizing its abortion policy over many years, the Romanian government in 1957 legalized abortion on request. The number of abortions rose quickly, so that by 1959, the last year for which relatively complete statistics are available, there were approximately 60 abortions for every 100 live births. This policy was reversed in 1966—in order to protect the health of women and to reduce concern over the decline in the birth rate, according to official explanations. Several additional policies were also enacted to encourage births. In 1969 family allowances were liberalized and increased, while in the same year the income tax was reduced by 30 per cent for families with three or more children. A "childlessness" tax was reintroduced and levied on men and women over

26 years of age whether married or single. The basis on which the government paid a birth allowance was also changed in 1966 to favor more births.[5] The accompanying figure illustrates both the dramatic, short-run impact of government abortion and tax policies, and also the steady subsequent dissipation of this impact over time.

GOVERNMENT POLICY

Apart from such direct efforts to affect fertility through official policies and laws, many governments have used propaganda to further the ideal of either a large or small family. The efforts of the Brazilian government to encourage the large family ideal "in the interests of national security" represent one extreme. Many countries, however, have recently turned to policies that support reduced population growth. Mexico, for instance, abruptly reversed its position in mid-1972, announcing that it planned to establish a nationwide network of family planning clinics with the purpose of stabilizing its population as soon as possible.

In China, population policies have vacillated over the past twenty-three years of the Communist regime between the position that problems of rapid population growth did not exist in a socialist society and recognition that high population growth rates posed a serious threat to future well-being. In recent years, the latter view has prevailed. Indeed, China now has one of the most aggressive programs to slow population growth of any country in the world. This has been well illustrated by Luke T. Lee, who cites the following admonitions from a 1966 Chinese calendar:

> On the eighth day of the month, the calendar cautioned that a large family would affect adversely not only the quality of work, production and study, but also the health of parents and children; hence the people should practice birth control. On the 12th day it reminded the reader that those needing abortion could go to any hospital for operations with all expenses taken care of by the government. On the 18th day, the calendar urged late marriages—women should not marry before 24 years of age, nor men before 28—in the interest of learning, raising the political, cultural, and skill levels, and serving the cause of socialism.[6]

It should be noted that these efforts to reduce family size are directly linked to opportunities to improve the welfare of the individual and the community. Such efforts are likely to be effective only when the people themselves perceive that such opportunities are actually available. Thus success is keyed to extension of opportunities for improvement to the entire population.

NEW INSTITUTIONS TO
PROVIDE SOCIAL SECURITY

In addition to government policies that have a direct impact on fertility, a number of other types of changes in a society also may stimulate decisions to limit births. These changes can be effected by either private or governmental action—and of course may be adopted for reasons other than their relationship to fertility.

In less developed countries, parents often desire to have large families in order to be sure of having children who will support them during old age. Alternative sources of social security can eliminate extreme economic dependence on children. As such systems become sufficiently stable for parents to rely on them, the importance of having a large family is likely to decline.

The Chinese "production team" is one example of a new social institution that may in time generate the financial and social security formerly provided by a strong family structure. Under this system, well-being in old age is influenced little, if at all, by the number of a couple's children. Goods produced by the team and income earned from marketed output are usually allocated among members of the team according to the number of points awarded for work. However, the problem of how much of the team's product and income should go to the "dependent population," principally the aged, has not yet been totally resolved.

SMALL FAMILY INCENTIVE PROGRAMS

In the last few years, several programs to provide incentives for parents to limit their family size have been considered and experimented with in a number of developing countries. One of these, a "savings account for family planning," was designed by Ronald Ridker and is now being tried in the very special institutional setting of the tea estates of India. The tea estates are already required by law to provide substantial maternity and child care benefits. These include not only hospitalization and medical care for the mother and infant, but also long-term food, clothing, schooling, and medical care for the child. Good vital records, hospitals, family clinics, and doctors are available on all of the estates.

Under the savings scheme, the tea estate management offers each woman of child-bearing age a savings account into which it will pay a specified amount for each month that the woman is not pregnant. The woman employee makes no payments into the account, but she is not eligible to withdraw the savings until her child-bearing years are over. The total cash savings that the woman ultimately receives depend on the age at which she becomes a participant and on how faithfully she keeps her half of the commitment. If she does become pregnant, the company ceases payments for a specified period and also reclaims part of its past payments into her account. These retroactive deductions are graduated according to the number of the woman's additional births, and are reclaimed by the company to help defray its expenses for these births. The response to the program over the first few months—including participation of 94 per cent of the eligible women—suggests that the system is well-suited for its institutional and social environment.

What the tea estates are in effect doing is offering their women employees a choice. They can continue to receive the maternity and health care benefits to which they are entitled. Or, by deciding to limit family size, they can opt to receive roughly the same benefits in the form of savings for their retirement and old age. This approach can be adapted to other settings—provided that these also offer easy and cheap access to locally acceptable contraceptive methods, an efficient administrative structure, and comprehension of the offered scheme on the part of those eligible to participate.[7]

Other new social security schemes designed to reduce the need for having large families are now being tried and considered elsewhere. The Malaysian government is debating a proposal that would make assistance for the aged available only for those parents with fewer than three children. In Taiwan, where the penchant for education is particularly strong, the government is experimenting with a bond system that will provide support for the advanced education of students in families with no more than three children. The risk with any such proposal, however, is that, as long as the poor tend to have more children than the rich, additional benefits may be transferred to the rich, thus further institutionalizing inequities.

Many types of "welfare programs" have been suggested to help alleviate the problems of the poor while at the same time affecting family size. Economic incentives for adopting birth control measures are an example. Such programs raise numerous ethical as well as social and economic questions, however; economic rewards may, for instance, greatly attract the poor while not affecting the rest of society. Wherever the poor represent a distinct religious, racial, or ethnic group, such incentive programs bring up the issue of implicit or explicit control over family size of a particular group.

In addition to the moral questions raised, there is the very basic pragmatic question of how best to create an environment in which people will voluntarily decide to limit family size in the broader social interest. If the poor continue to have many children, and they are in turn penalized economically for having a large family, then their children are likely to become trapped in the same kind of poverty that will again prevent them from practicing family planning. It is precisely those families with many children that have the greatest need to receive special social and financial benefits if their next generation is to be motivated to limit family size.

THE STATUS OF WOMEN

Another factor that can have a major impact on desired family size is an improvement in the status of women. This change is often an integral part of the development process; as the economy expands, women become better educated and more involved in economic and political processes. Although certain elements of this increased activity function as a "dependent variable" and will emerge simply through their relationship to other changes in the society, other developments that may be adopted independently can have a substantial impact on the development process itself.

When the relative position of women in society changes and they are given more equal educational opportunities, the chance is improved that they will delay marriage and also practice contraception once they are married. If women are granted equal employment opportunities, and rewarded equally for their work, many will reorient their adult activities to take advantage of work opportunities, thus reducing the relative importance of child-bearing. The increased participation of women in the modern social and political system generally helps to bring about the transition to reduced family size.

CHILD LABOR AND COMPULSORY EDUCATION

Child labor practices and compulsory or universal education also have indirect effects on fertility. It was noted earlier that children who go to school instead of working are likely to be regarded by their parents as financial liabilities, rather than assets, at least during their youth. In his report on "Law and Family Planning," Luke T. Lee points out that the great majority of countries now have some laws for compulsory education—although studies conducted by UNESCO indicate marked differences between law and fact. Lee's study also notes that "the principle of prohibiting child labor is now almost universally accepted," although once again, the principle is often not enforced.[8] In most developing countries, it is impractical to expect enforcement of either of these laws. However, to the extent that the laws do spread educational opportunities, as well as limit the opportunities for employment of child labor on a broad scale, they will have an impact on the demographic transition of many countries.

SELECTIVE DISTRIBUTION

Still another way to affect fertility without addressing the problems of the entire socio-economic continuum is to aim government support at just those factors that appear to be most closely related to reducing fertility.[9] Widespread distribution of just a few, specific services, such as the education of women, child health services, nutrition programs, and birth control information and supplies may cause a reduction of births without "penalizing" large families or transferring additional resources to the small, relatively rich families. Such specific measures do not, however, promise to stimulate the "cumulative effect" of broadly-based distribution policies such as those described in Chapter II, and can only be expected to bring about a rather limited decline in births.

family planning
in the broader framework

The increased interest and concern that population problems have
aroused in recent years has been reflected in the spread of family
planning and population programs. Generally, population policy is
taken to mean support for clinics providing family planning services, but it certainly relates as well to the concept of improving
the quality of life for the entire population. In the latter sense,
most of this paper may be considered relevant to a national population policy. Even within the narrower category of family
planning programs, objectives range from simply limiting births to
improving health care for the entire family. In the broader sense,
the introduction of family planning programs is a new and important development variable that should be treated as a part of an
integrated approach to socio-economic development.

47

Family planning programs make available the easier and better means for limiting births. To limit family size, however, individuals must acquire not only the means, but also the motivation
to do so. Within limits, there is a trade-off between motivation and
means, and an increase in either will provide at least a short-term
reduction in births. In two societies with equal motivation, the
one in which family planning services are more readily available
will experience the more rapid decline in birth rates.

The effect of family planning programs on fertility has not
been satisfactorily measured. It is extremely difficult to separate
out the partial effect of such programs from the overall effect of
other social and economic changes. In the case of Korea, for example, it has been estimated that family planning programs account, at most, for about one-third of the sharp decline in births
that has occurred in the last decade.[1] Some of the reports on the
initial experience of the Philippines with family planning suggest
that acceptance has been particularly high among those farm families which have improved their economic situation through the
"green revolution." There are still other problems with measuring
the direct effects of family planning programs. Where birth control
is strongly encouraged by financial and other incentives, reports of

rapid initial rates of adoption may not be indicative of a permanent change in practice.

Moreover, in the long run, family planning programs tend to have what may be called a "once-and-for-all" effect on fertility—as a population moves from no knowledge or access to modern contraceptive methods to complete knowledge and access. Thus in Taiwan, family planning programs initially spread rapid acceptance of contraceptives; after a five-year period, however, much of the country was saturated with the requisite information and the marginal cost of preventing each additional birth went up sharply—nearly twentyfold by one estimate.[2]

Most of the less developed countries, however, are still far short of being "saturated" with birth control information. In some of these countries, including the Philippines, Thailand, and Indonesia, major family planning efforts are still too new to be reliably assessed. It is nevertheless reasonable to expect that these programs will be helpful in coping with the problems of the less developed countries caused by rapid population growth. On the basis of what is known about the effectiveness of family planning programs thus far, however, they certainly cannot be considered as a panacea for the complex set of problems related to population and development facing the poor countries.

A clearer understanding of the effects of social and economic development on attitudes toward child-bearing—a central objective of this paper—can provide a framework for assessing the prospects for successful family planning programs in different settings. Both experience and the limited studies made to date suggest that family planning programs are most effective when accompanied by social and economic development. Examples of the case histories of three programs in India, which has now experimented with family planning programs for over twenty years, illustrate the effectiveness of family planning programs in different socio-economic circumstances.

In the first of these cases, a family planning program tested in the 1950s had virtually no effect on birth rates. Several villages in the rural Punjab were carefully studied by a Harvard research team between 1953 and 1960. In some of the villages ("test" villages), family planning information and birth control devices—in the forms available in the 1950s—were regularly provided. In others ("control" villages), these services were not made available. The study showed no decline of any significance in the birth rates of either the test or the control villages over that period. Yet when the research group that had conducted the first study returned to study the use of contraceptives in the same area a decade later, in 1969, it found that the birth rate had declined in *all* of the villages. This decline in fertility coincided with the marked improvements in socio-economic conditions—higher agricultural yields and better health and education services—experienced in the Punjab in the 1960s.[3]

Elsewhere in India as well as in some other developing countries, cash incentives combined with efficient administration have been largely responsible for increased acceptance of family planning programs. Perhaps the most dramatic of these examples is the experience of the Ernakulum District of the state of Kerala, where a family planning "festival" was held in July of 1971 in which 63,000 men obtained vasectomies.[4] Each man who agreed to the operation was provided free transportation and given goods worth about $12, along with a lottery ticket. People who referred participants to the festival were also rewarded. The unprecedented rate of acceptance appears to have been due to a combination of factors: 1) the district's relatively high rates of literacy and mobility, 2) the fact that Ernakulum is the most industrialized district in the state, 3) extremely overcrowded conditions, 4) high responsiveness to cash incentives, and 5) efficient administration. This program illustrates one workable approach to reduced fertility. But questions as to its transferability and the extent of its effect on pre-existing attitudes toward family planning are left unresolved. Moreover, such programs raise some difficult questions concerning public and individual moral responsibility.

In general, villages that have experienced rapid improvements in living standards have also led the way in birth rate reductions. The village of Narangwal of the Ludhiana District, which leads the Indian Punjab in agricultural development, is a striking example of the beginning of a decline in birth rates. In this locality, family planning has been integrated with health services. Concurrent advances have been made in education and economic status. The cumulative effect of appropriate development strategies—with family planning as one component—is working in Ludhiana. What is of special interest is that parents are choosing to have smaller families despite the fact that average annual income remains below $150. According to Carl Taylor, who participated both in the Narangwal study and in the earlier rural Punjab study cited above, "Narangwal is atypical in that it has begun to change. It may, nevertheless, serve as a prototype of what can happen and so provide a basis for predicting a pattern of development for hundreds of thousands of villages in many parts of the world."[5]

49

It appears that once individuals reach a high level on the development-fertility continuum, they begin to use whatever means are available to limit births *whether or not birth control devices are provided.* A clear signal of the need for contraceptive services is the wide-scale resort to illegal, induced abortions. Although attitudes and laws concerning abortion have made reliable measurement very difficult, there does appear to be a relationship between socio-economic changes and the rise in demand for abortion. As Abdel Omran has suggested, "when developing societies are highly motivated to accelerate their transition from high to low fertility, induced abortion becomes such a popular method of fertility control that it becomes a kind of epidemic."[6]

South Korea, Colombia, Uruguay, and Argentina provide examples of different social settings in which apparent demand for abortion suggests that family planning programs are likely to be particularly effective. In South Korea, rapid socio-economic changes have had a major impact on a large part of the population. The birth rate has dropped sharply in the last decade. Although illegal, abortions are widely performed by physicians with very little interference from the government. According to a recent study, induced abortion in Korea has increased by 72 per cent in the past six years. It has been estimated that among women between the ages of 20 and 44, 43 per cent had aborted at least one pregnancy by 1970.[7] Studies conducted in Latin America show similar trends, despite much stronger religious and legal constraints. A study on induced abortions in Colombia notes that, "the prevalence of abortions is higher in urban areas than in rural areas, and decidedly greater in more developed urban sectors than in less developed ones. An inverse ratio exists between the degree of primitivism of a community and the prevalence of abortions."[8] In Argentina and Uruguay—where the great majority of the population has shared in the substantial benefits of earlier economic and social progress, and where birth rates are the lowest in South America despite the only very limited availability of family planning programs—the ratios of illegal abortion are high. In Uruguay, the abortion rate is estimated at three per live birth.[9]

The preceding examples illustrate the usefulness of family planning. In India, some family planning programs have been designed to reinforce the desire to limit births as soon as it exists. In some cases, incentives have been offered to encourage that decision. In others, family planning programs have been integrated with health and education services—a combination that appears to encourage limitation of family size. In still other countries, such as Korea, family planning programs are part of an effort to bring birth control services to those who, through high abortion rates, have already expressed a desire to limit births. In Colombia, where urban abortion rates are high, the desire to limit family size clearly exists in the wealthier communities, as it does on a broader basis in the generally better-off societies of Argentina and Uruguay. There is an urgent need for greatly expanded family planning services in such settings merely to protect the health of women and to meet existing demand for such services.

Especially when combined with other social services, family planning can have a very positive effect on the health and welfare of the population. It is, moreover, a *social service*, not just a means to limit births. It should be noted that in most societies, the wealthy *already* have much greater access to family planning services than do the poor. Family planning services should be distributed throughout the population in a manner consistent with other services to improve well-being.

The effectiveness of family planning programs should be enhanced by their integration with other efforts to expand access to the modern social system, and their distribution to the entire population should be assigned high priority. Such an integrated approach will offer families both the means and the motivation to limit births.

toward a comprehensive
development-population strategy

Few would disagree that in the 1970s we need to relieve the 51
pressures of rapid population growth on man himself and on his
natural environment. From some perspectives, the population explosion threatens the "limits" of the world's resources. There is
still no consensus as to when these limits will be reached, or even
what their meaning is in terms of the quality of our lives. But it is
quite clear that rapid population growth is straining not only the
standard of living and the distribution of services within the developing countries, but also certain aspects of relations between the
affluent and the poor countries.

This study shows that there is a close and very important
relationship between socio-economic development and population
growth. On the basis of historical trends and recent experience in
developing countries, it argues that when a broad cross-section of
the population in developing countries benefits sufficiently from
development—and apparently not before then—the motivation for
smaller families is greatly increased and population growth significantly slowed. It seems that when the physical, economic, and
social conditions of their lives are improved, people act to limit
family size. In these circumstances, family planning programs can
play their most effective role.

Research on the correlation between socio-economic development and motivation for smaller families is still at an early stage
and calls for much greater refinement, but the current level of
analysis already provides some useful policy guidelines for both
the developing and the rich countries.

For the developing countries, the findings of this study quite
clearly point to adopting those strategies which—while using the
present level of available resources—will deal with the problems of
poverty, unemployment, poor health, malnutrition, and lack of
educational opportunities more directly and enable the greatest
possible number of people to reach a socio-economic level conducive to family planning. Such strategies vary in different settings, as Chapter II of this study indicates, but lessons can be

gleaned from the experience of countries that appear to have implemented this approach successfully.

A ROLE FOR THE U.S.
AND OTHER DEVELOPED COUNTRIES

While the most basic initiatives and decisions relating to both poverty and population growth must necessarily be made by the particular poor nations concerned, the policies of the rich nations of the world clearly can affect the progress of the poor countries along the development-fertility continuum described in this study.

The rich countries—and particularly the United States—can play an extremely useful research and support role in this area. An outstanding example of what such outside assistance can do was provided by the sequence of external efforts that led to the "green revolution": the early identification of the food crisis of the mid-1960s, followed by the work of the Rockefeller and Ford Foundations in developing new high-yielding grain seeds, and the subsequent large-scale financial support by the U.S. Agency for International Development and other organizations to facilitate the massive introduction of these new seeds in many countries. External assistance clearly played a very important role in bringing about the "green revolution."

In the case of the global population problem, too, the developed countries, particularly the United States, have already made a significant contribution. Much valuable work has been carried out to improve birth control techniques, and considerable financial support has been forthcoming for family planning programs in those poor countries that have requested foreign assistance to make such programs available to their populations. More such support is needed to complement efforts to deal with global poverty.

But this study maintains that there is also a further urgent need for a major research program to identify more specifically the relationship of different variables in the development process—such as education or employment—to the *motivation* for smaller families. The developed countries could make a major contribution in this area.

Moreover, if the global population explosion is to be effectively checked, the United States and other developed countries must launch far more vigorous efforts on two other principal fronts. *First*, there is a need for a major increase in the transfer of resources from rich countries to poor to help the latter accelerate development. It is no accident that most of the development—and family planning—"success stories" have taken place in societies with broad access to external resources. But there must be major changes in the ways rich countries relate to the poor countries if there is to be anything like the needed increase in the transfer of resources in the 1970s. Additional sources of foreign exchange must come from trade, investment, aid, and possibly, from such new global sources as the raw materials of the seabed and the foreign exchange made available by the International Monetary Fund through the Special Drawing Rights mechanism. *Second*, the developed countries must attempt to ensure that the transfer of resources from them to poor countries increasingly takes place in ways that facilitate rather than deter attempts to improve distribution and employment patterns in the less developed countries.

A NEW DIMENSION FOR AID

Direct foreign assistance has made a contribution to increases in output in the developing countries in recent years. But the track record of the aid programs of the developed countries has been mixed if evaluated in terms of the distribution of their benefits within the recipient countries. In some cases, the transfer of capital and technical assistance has taken place in ways that facilitate broad distribution and high employment. But in others, aid programs have led to inappropriate, capital-intensive investments that created few jobs and further distorted the distribution of national income.

The initiative for development programs must come from the governments of the countries desiring them—since foreign assistance does not generally involve the power to decide what will be done with the funds provided, but only which of the recommended programs will be funded. When asked to do so, however, the rich countries *can* assist in building those institutions that will favorably affect the distribution of income. Land reform, credit institutions, and cooperatives are among the elements of such an approach. The rich countries can provide support for the development of those social services that are likely to have a more direct impact on living conditions, and hence on population growth. Effective support should be provided for programs giving all women and men access at least to a primary level of education and to rudimentary health services. Health and educational services should be widely distributed to the entire population. Care should be taken to not simply export Western health and education systems, but rather to encourage the development of programs more suited to local conditions. To develop applicable systems of health care and education, both rich and poor countries should begin a systematic review of some of the more successful programs in these areas that are already in operation in countries as ideologically different as Ceylon, Taiwan, and China.

Those assistance-program practices that adversely affect the investment decisions of the developing nations should certainly be avoided. Tying aid to purchases in the donor country and refusing to permit it to be used for local expenses can cause the recipient to import capital-intensive machinery and equipment—the wrong approach, since it creates few jobs. All such practices should be viewed critically in terms of whether they will quickly and appreciably increase benefits for the poor.

Finally, expanded support for research on improved birth control techniques and for family planning programs is crucial if rapid population growth is to be reduced. For several reasons, however, it is important not to provide such services to the exclusion of other development support. To do so would give the mistaken impression that the United States and other developed countries are interested only in the "numbers" of men and women in developing countries, not in the quality of their lives. Unfortunately, this impression has helped to arouse opposition in many developing countries to the introduction and expansion of population programs.

It is therefore important, for psychological as well as substantive reasons, that the U.S. government adopt population policies that reflect a genuine awareness of the relationship between population problems and other needs of the developing countries. The current rapid increase in support for family planning programs should be accompanied by appropriate improvements in the broader trade, monetary, and aid relationships that make major contributions to living standards, and hence, as this study argues, to the motivation for smaller families.

REFORM OF THE INTERNATIONAL ECONOMIC SYSTEM

Direct foreign assistance provided by the United States and other rich countries cannot alone be regarded as adequate to provide the resources now needed by the poor countries in solving their pressing problems of economic development. Yet without progress toward the solution of these problems, there is little chance of greatly changing the rate of population growth. Together with other rich countries, the United States should begin to search for new ways to increase the transfer of real resources to the poor countries. This will, perforce, require changes in the international economic system itself. Originally designed by the rich countries with primarily their own needs in mind, this system currently provides less than equal treatment for the more than two-thirds of the world's people who are poor.

The international trade mechanism and the world monetary system provide two cases in point. The Kennedy Round of tariff negotiations of the 1960s, for example, reduced the tariffs on goods traded between the rich countries by half. But it did almost nothing to reduce the tariffs on goods from the poor countries, and thus left these countries relatively worse off than before. This situation has been exacerbated by the great increase in non-tariff barriers on products from the poor countries. The advanced industrial countries are currently struggling to subsidize inefficient domestic industries that use relatively unskilled labor. In effect, however, the price of such policies is paid by the workers in the poor countries and the consumers in the rich countries. A wiser long-run course would be to create an effective set of domestic employment and adjustment assistance policies. Combined with a fairer trade policy, such measures could benefit labor in the United States while helping to meet the needs of the poor countries for more foreign exchange and more jobs.[1]

The needs of the developing countries should also be upgraded on the agenda of the current negotiations on international monetary reform. In 1969 the members of the International Monetary Fund agreed to create "paper gold"—new international liquidity in the form of Special Drawing Rights—amounting to more than $9 billion over a three-year period. Under the distribution formula agreed upon at that time, nearly three-quarters of this new reserve asset was made available to the 25 richest countries and only the remaining quarter to the 87 participating poor nations—whose development is critically dependent on their ability to obtain foreign exchange. More recently, not only the equitability, but also the efficiency of this SDR distribution formula have increasingly come to be questioned. It is argued that its reform holds potential advantages for both rich and poor countries: it could be helpful in reducing barriers to trade, in reconciling the conflicting trade goals of the major developed countries, and in encouraging the poor countries to follow sound economic policies.[2]

As the United States and other rich countries confront these and other new issues in trade, monetary, and resource policies, they must continually seek to identify those approaches which, while beneficial to themselves, will also facilitate rather than deter the development of the poor countries.

THE NEED FOR RESEARCH

The United States and other developed countries can make a further important contribution to alleviating the poverty-population crisis by strengthening relevant research and development efforts within the rich countries—an area in which the United States in particular has an overwhelming comparative advantage. Research is now under way, and should be continued, to develop effective contraceptives appropriate to the conditions of the poor countries. But data collection and research analysis in the poor countries concerning the relationship between population and development also should be greatly increased and should aim toward improving our ability to promote human welfare. This calls for better understanding of the interaction between the social, economic, and demographic variables involved in the development process of the poor countries. Cooperation among economists and social scientists may lead to important breakthroughs in our understanding of these relationships.

Finally, there is a need for research on a vast range of subjects that will affect the development of the poor countries. To cite only one example, many existing technologies in the rich countries were created in response to the need to save labor; yet labor continues to be the most abundant national resource of many of the poor countries. With the same spirit and energy that marked their support of the research that produced the "green revolution," the rich countries should now undertake support of research in other areas vital to the development of the poor countries. Such research efforts should assign special priority to the need to devise delivery systems for health and education services that are more appropriate to the limited means of developing countries.

CONCLUSIONS

The central proposition derived from this study is that, in the 1970s development planners need to give far more attention than heretofore to the *effect of alternative development strategies on birth rates*. Equally important, those decision-makers concerned with alleviating population problems need to think of remedies for the population crisis in the larger context of the development crisis—to consider the possible ways of treating the basic "disease" of poverty and, by doing so, creating the needed motivation for smaller families. Policies that bring health, education, and mean-

55

ingful jobs to lower income groups can at the same time contribute toward reducing population growth and accelerating economic growth, and can thus provide a solid base on which to build future development policies. These policies, when combined with large-scale, well-executed family planning programs, should make it possible to stabilize a developing country's population much more rapidly than reliance on either approach alone.

Even if more effective ways are found to limit births—even if a perfect contraceptive is devised and made readily available—other problems of development must still be addressed. While the better distribution of opportunities for improvement has been represented as an approach that is likely to reduce population growth, it is also likely to reduce malnutrition, poor health, and unemployment. This complementary relationship is more than just incidental; it is key both to the adoption of appropriate policies and to making available the financial resources needed for such policies. There is still much to be learned about the direct relationship between the distribution of opportunities and overall birth rate reduction. There is sufficient evidence, however, to understand the basic direction that policies should take. Although there is certainly no sign of easy "solutions," it is possible to move ahead on policies that are of basic importance to the improvement of human welfare. "Growth with justice" may well be an indispensable key to the reduction and eventual stabilization of population growth.

While none of the proposals set forth in this study will be easy to put into practice, they will be easier to launch now than later. The pressures of population growth are inexorably increasing. By beginning now it may be possible to reduce, or even stabilize, population growth at a much lower overall level than if another decade is allowed to pass before effective action is taken.

footnotes

CHAPTER I

[1]Donald Bogue, *Principles of Demography* (New York: John Wiley and 57
Sons, 1969), p. 55. Professor Bogue emphasizes, however, that "the theory of
demographic transition is not intended to be a detailed and refined 'law of
population growth,' but is only an empirical generalization of the world's
demographic history."

[2]Ulla Olin, "A Note on Historical Birth and Death Rates and Population Growth," in M. L. Qureshi, ed., "Population Growth and Economic
Development," summary report of a seminar organized by the Institute of
Development Economics, Karachi, Pakistan, in cooperation with the Population Council, New York, September 1959.

[3]Dudley Kirk, "A New Demographic Transition," in *Rapid Population
Growth, Consequences and Policy Implications*, Vol. II (Baltimore: Johns
Hopkins University Press, 1971), p. 133. Published for the National Academy
of Sciences.

[4]United Nations, *Population Bulletin* 7, 1963, p. 144 (published in
1965).

[5]An estimate of the current U.S. gross reproduction rate, for example,
is 1.2, or just slightly higher than one female child per woman of reproductive
age. In India, the gross reproduction rate is 2.7, indicating an average of
nearly 3 daughters per woman of reproductive age.

[6]The Research Triangle Institute has reviewed many of the studies in
this area, most recently in *Social and Economic Correlates of Family Fertility: An Updated Review of the Evidence*, by Norman H. Loewenthal and
Abraham S. David (prepared for Asia Bureau/Office of Population Programs,
June 1972). The different studies reflect the wide variations in available
information. The country that probably has the best available data and that
has been studied most is Taiwan.

Studies by the Rand Corporation have reported on available data from
the Latin American and Asian regions. See T. Paul Schultz, *Demographic
Conditions of Economic Development in Latin America* (Santa Monica:
Rand, 1968); Marc Nerlove and T. Paul Schultz, *Love and Life
Between the Censuses: A Model of Family Decision Making in Puerto Rico,
1950-1960* (Santa Monica: Rand, 1970); Alvin Harman, *Fertility and Eco-
nomic Behavior of Families in the Philippines* (Santa Monica: Rand, 1970);
Julie DaVanzo, *The Determinants of Family Formation in Chile, 1960: An
Econometric Study of Female Labor Force Participation, Marriage, and Fer-
tility Decisions* (Santa Monica: Rand, 1972).

The Latin American Demographic Center (CELADE) has collected data
that allow for comparative studies of rural and urban areas in Mexico, Chile,
Brazil, and Colombia. See Carmen Miro and Walter Mertens, "Influences Af-

fecting Fertility in Urban and Rural Latin America," *Milbank Memorial Fund Quarterly* 46, no. 3 (July 1968), pp. 89-117.

In much of Africa, data are still too scarce for thorough analysis. See Julian Condé, *The Demographic Transition as Applied to Tropical Africa, with Particular Reference to Health, Education, and Economic Factors* (Paris: OECD Development Centre, August 1971).

[7] Ansley Coale, "The Decline of Fertility in Europe from the French Revolution to World War II," in S. J. Behrman, Leslie Corsa, Jr., and Ronald Freedman, eds., *Fertility and Family Planning: A World View* (Ann Arbor: University of Michigan Press, 1969), p. 18.

[8] See T. Paul Schultz, "An Economic Perspective on Population Growth," in *Rapid Population Growth, Consequences, and Policy Implications, op. cit.*, p. 162.

[9] See Everett M. Rogers and F. Floyd Shoemaker, *Communication of Innovations, A Cross-Cultural Approach* (New York: The Free Press, 1971), pp. 241 and 286.

[10] See Deborah Freedman, "The Relation of Economic Status to Fertility," *American Economic Review* 53 (June 1963), pp. 414-26; Nerlove and Schultz, *op. cit.*; Miro and Mertens, *op. cit.*; or Harman, *op. cit.*

[11] Eva Mueller, "Agricultural Change and Fertility Changes" (University of Michigan Population Studies Center, 1971), p. 34.

[12] See Carl Taylor, "Population Trends in an Indian Village," *Scientific American* 223, no. 1 (July 1970); and Carl Taylor and Marie-Francoise Hall, "Health, Population and Economic Development," *Science* 157, August 11, 1967, pp. 651-57.

[13] David Heer and Dean O. Smith, "Mortality Level and Desired Family Size," in *Contributed Papers of the Sydney Conference of the International Union for the Scientific Study of Population*, 1967, pp. 26-36.

[14] David Heer and David May, "Son Survivorship Motivation and Family Size in India: A Computer Simulation," *Population Studies* 22, no. 2 (1968), p. 206.

[15] T. Paul Schultz, "Retrospective Evidence of a Decline of Fertility and Child Mortality in Central East Pakistan," *Demography*, August 1972.

[16] S. Hassan, "Influence of Child Mortality on Fertility," paper presented at the annual meeting of The Population Association of America, New York, April 1966.

[17] Miro and Mertens, *op. cit.*, p. 96.

[18] Research Triangle Institute, *Social and Economic Correlates of Family Fertility: A Survey of the Evidence* (prepared for Near East-South Asia/Office of Population Programs, September 1971), p. 41; and Jerzy Berent, "Causes of Fertility Decline in Eastern Europe and the Soviet Union," *Population Studies* 24, nos. 1 and 2 (1970), pp. 247-54.

[19] Deborah S. Freedman, "Consumption of Modern Goods and Services and their Relation to Fertility: A Study in Taiwan." Unpublished paper prepared with support from the Population Council and the Population Studies Center at the University of Michigan, 1972.

[20] Godfrey Gunatilleke, "Rural-Urban Balance and Development: The Experience in Ceylon," paper prepared for a Southeast Asia Development Advisory Group Seminar on Population and Development, Thailand, June 1972. See also T. Paul Schultz, *Population Growth and Internal Migration in Colombia* (Santa Monica: Rand, 1969). This discussion of urbanization should not imply that urbanization is not an effective means of increasing access to goods and services and thus a means of reducing births.

[21] See p. 13.

[22] Mueller, *op. cit.,* pp. 24 and 31.

[23] See Annex A, p. 67, for figures 1) correlating the per capita income of the poorest 60 per cent of the population and the birth rate in 40 developing countries, and 2) correlating the per capita income of the entire population and the birth rate in 40 developing countries.

[24] Several economists have studied this question. See Stanley Friedlander and Morris Silver, "A Quantitative Study of the Determinants of Fertility Behavior," *Demography* 4 (1967), pp. 30-70; and Research Triangle Institute, *A Survey, op. cit.* Both studies indicate that there is a relationship

between income and fertility at different levels of development. In developed nations, fertility rises as income rises. In the poor countries, fertility declines with rises in income. Julian Simon has focused directly on this question. He notes that "in underdeveloped countries the unconditional effect of income on fertility is negative (fertility-reducing), even though its partial effect (after abstracting from other operative variables) may well be positive." See "The Effect of Income on Fertility," *Population Studies* 23 (November 1969), pp. 327 and 334. Simon also notes that this thesis is particularly relevant for the majority of the population in the poor countries subsisting at extremely low income levels, since a development program that leads to an increase in income for this group will lead to immediate improvements in basic necessities such as health, education, and nutrition. Thus, the overall effect of rises in income will be a reduction in births.

[25]James Kocher's study correlates income distribution patterns with fertility declines. See James E. Kocher, *Rural Development, Income Distribution, and Fertility Decline* (New York: The Population Council, in preparation). A summary table from Kocher's study, highlighting the importance of the distribution factor is included as *Annex B*, p. 68. For an analysis of the countries selected according to this criterion, see Edgar Owens and Robert Shaw, *Development Reconsidered* (Lexington, Mass.: D.C. Heath, 1972); and Kocher, *op. cit.*

[26]See Miro and Mertens, *op. cit.*, pp. 111-13; and Research Triangle Institute, *A Survey, op. cit.*

[27]For data on Mauritius, see Christo Xenos, "Mauritius," *Country Profiles* (September 1970). Published by the Population Council.

[28]T. Paul Schultz, *Fertility Patterns and their Determinants in the Arab Middle East* (Santa Monica: Rand, 1971), p. 45.

[29]T. N. Carver, *The Economy of Human Energy* (New York: Macmillan Company, 1924), p. 34.

[30]Several economists have considered parental decisions in terms of a range of alternatives associated with appropriate costs and benefits. Richard Easterlin has studied fertility choices along with a range of household economic decisions in the United States. See "Toward a Socioeconomic Theory of Fertility: A Survey of Recent Research on Economic Factors in American Fertility," in Behrman, Corsa, and Freedman, *op. cit.* Dennis De Tray has studied the alternatives between a few well educated and cared for children, and a larger family with a smaller investment per child. See *An Economic Analysis of Quantity-Quality Substitution in Household Fertility Decisions* (Santa Monica: Rand, 1970); and *The Interaction Between Parent Investment in Children and Family Size: An Economic Analysis* (Santa Monica: Rand, 1972). Although most such studies so far have been confined to U.S. data, their basic premises, and the conclusions reached, may have great significance when the impact of such new household alternatives is studied in societies where they previously were not available or were not perceived to be within reach of the average individual.

[31]Kocher, *op. cit.*

[32]Edgardo Mascardi, "Mexico, Study of Plan Puebla" (Master's Thesis, Centro Economia Agricola, Escuela Nacional de Agricultura, Chapingo, Mexico, 1972).

[33]James R. Hooker, "Population Planning in Rhodesia, 1971," *American University Fieldstaff Reports*, Central and Southern Africa Series 15, no. 6 (July 1971).

[34]Theodore Hesburgh, "A Concerned Catholic," *The New York Times*, April 20, 1972, section 12, p. 11.

[35]A. Majee Khan and Harvey M. Chaldin, "New Family Planners in Rural East Pakistan," *Demography* 2 (1965), pp. 1-7. Visid Prachuabmoh, "Factors Affecting Desire or Lack of Desire for Additional Progeny in Thailand," in Donald Bogue, ed., *Sociological Contributions to Family Planning Research* (Chicago: Community and Family Study Center, 1967). References to both the Thailand and Bangladesh programs are included in Bogue, *Principles of Demography*, pp. 843-47.

[36]"Mass Vasectomy Camp of Garakhpur Division," prepared by the State Family Planning Bureau, Uttar Pradesh, India, 1972.

[1] Irma Adelman and Cynthia Taft Morris have also noted that: "Once a sharply dualistic development pattern has been initiated, further economic growth actually *reduces* the share of the lowest 60 per cent. When the dualistic development pattern is primarily foreign managed and financed, higher GNP tends to lower the share of the middle income households as well." See "An Anatomy of Income Distribution Patterns in Developing Nations," *Development Digest*, October 1971, p. 37.

[2] See Mahbub ul Haq, "Employment in the 1970's: A New Perspective," *International Development Review* 13, no. 4 (1971).

[3] See Robert McNamara, "Address to the United Nations Conference on Trade and Development," Santiago, Chile, April 14, 1972 (Washington, D.C.: International Bank for Reconstruction and Development, 1972), p. 4.

[4] David Turnham, "Income Distribution: Measurement and Problems," in Andrew E. Rice, ed., *International Development 1971: Development Targets for the 70's: Jobs and Justice* (Dobbs Ferry, N.Y.: Oceana Publications, 1972), pp. 37-59.

[5] McNamara, *op. cit.*, p. 4.

[6] Harry T. Oshima, "The Time to Change to Labor-Intensive Policies is Now," *Ceres*, November-December 1970, p. 32.

[7] G. Tobias, *Human Resources Utilization and Development in the Seventies*, (New Delhi: The Ford Foundation, May 1970), pp. 3-4.

[8] Raúl Prebisch et. al., *Towards Full Employment* (A Programme for Colombia Prepared by an Inter-Agency Team Organized by the International Labour Organization, Geneva, 1970).

[9] ul Haq, *op. cit.*, p. 12.

[10] Robert Shaw, "Rethinking Economic Development," *Headline Series* 208 (December 1971). Published by the Foreign Policy Association, New York.

[11] For further discussion see Edgar Owens and Robert Shaw, *Development Reconsidered, op. cit.* See also Robert E. Hunter, James P. Grant, and William Rich, *A New Development Strategy: Greater Equity, Faster Growth, and Smaller Families*, Development Paper No. 11, Overseas Development Council. October 1972.

[12] ul Haq, *op. cit.*, p. 12.

[13] For a discussion of income distribution data and problems of measurement, see Simon Kuznets, "Quantitative Aspects of the Economic Growth of Nations: VIII, Distribution of Income by Size," *Economic Development and Cultural Change* 2 (January 1963); and Richard Weiskoff, "Income Distribution and Economic Growth in Puerto Rico, Argentina, and Mexico," *Review of Income and Wealth*, December 1970.

[14] Turnham, *op. cit.*, p. 11.

[15] Different political, social, and religious factors, as well as differences in health services and family planning programs should also be considered in a comparison of fertility in Taiwan and the Philippines. The focus of this discussion, however, is that different distributions have meant that the living conditions of the poor in Taiwan are much better than those of the poor in the Philippines. See also Annex C of this study, p. 70.

[16] U.S. Agency for International Development, "The Rationale for the Key Problem Areas," August 1971, p. 5. For further discussion of this topic, see Lee Howard, "Key Problems Impeding Modernization of Developing Countries: The Health Issues" (Washington, D.C.: AID, December 1970).

[17] Data from U.S. Agency for International Development *Economic Data Book: Near East and South Asia* (updated to December 1971).

[18] Korean Ministry of Health and Social Affairs, *Social Development*, 1970.

[19] See Leo A. Orleans, "China's Population Problems: Generation to Generation," *Foreign Service Journal*, February 1972, p. 23.

[20] Miro and Mertens, *op. cit.*, p. 107.

[21] Julius Nyerere, *Freedom and Unity* (Dar es Salaam, Tanzania: Oxford University Press, 1966), p. 316.

[22] Philip Coombs, "Opportunities in Nonformal Education for Rural Development," in Kenneth W. Thompson and F. Champion Ward, eds., *Edu-*

cation and Development Reconsidered, vol. 2 (prepared for a conference held at Villa Serbelloni, Bellagio, Italy, May 3-5, 1972, sponsored by the Ford and Rockefeller Foundations), p. 155.

[23] Owens and Shaw, *op. cit.*, p. 129.

[24] Alan Berg, "India Fortifies Its Children," *Washington Post*, July 12, 1970.

[25] Lester R. Brown, *Seeds of Change* (New York: Frederick A. Praeger, Inc., 1970), p. 114.

[26] Keith Marsden, "Progressive Technologies for Developing Countries," *International Labor Review* 101, no. 5 (May 1970), p. 481.

[27] Owens and Shaw, *op. cit.*, pp. 115-116.

[28] James P. Grant, "Jobs and Justice: Economic Growth Alone is not Enough," in *Development Today: A New Look at U.S. Relations With the Poor Countries* (New York: Praeger Publishers, Inc., 1972), p. 145.

[29] Owens and Shaw, *op. cit.*, p. 95.

[30] Keith Marsden, "Towards A Synthesis of Economic Growth and Social Justice," *International Labor Review* 100, no. 5 (November 1969), pp. 412-414.

[31] Academy for Rural Development, Comilla (Bangladesh), 9th Annual Report, "A New Rural Cooperative System for Comilla Thana, 1968-69."

[32] For a more complete table contrasting development indicators in South Korea, Taiwan, Brazil, Mexico, and the Philippines, see Annex C, p. 70.

61

CHAPTER III

[1] Dorothy Nortman, "Populations and Family Planning Programs: A Factbook," in *Reports on Population/Family Planning*, no. 2 (July 1971), p. 4.

[2] Luke T. Lee, "Law and Family Planning," *Studies in Family Planning* 2, no. 4 (April 1971), p. 82.

[3] Willard Hanna, "The Republic of Singapore: Population Review 1970," *American University Fieldstaff Reports*, Southeast Asia Series 19, no. 5 (1970), p. 23.

[4] Thomas Sanders, "The Politics of Population in Brazil," *American University Fieldstaff Reports*, East Coast South America Series 15, no. 1 (April 1970), p. 1.

[5] Henry David and Nicholas Wright, "Abortion Legislation: The Romanian Experience," *Studies in Family Planning* 2, no. 10 (October 1971), pp. 206-209.

[6] Lee, *op. cit.*, p. 94.

[7] Ronald Ridker, "Savings Accounts for Family Planning, An Illustration from the Tea Estates of India," *Studies in Family Planning* 2, no. 7 (July 1971), pp. 150-152.

[8] Lee, *op. cit.*, p. 90.

[9] James Tobin has analyzed a similar concept, which he termed "specific egalitarianism," as related to the U.S. economy. See "On Limiting the Domain of Inequity," *Journal of Law and Economics*, October 1970, p. 263. It would be useful to extend Tobin's analysis to the question of family size in the developing countries.

CHAPTER IV

[1] James Kocher, *op. cit.* p. 89.

[2] Paul Schultz has estimated that during that five-year period, the marginal cost of preventing each additional birth in Taiwan through the family planning program went up from $4 to $75. It should be noted, however, that along with increases in cost, there are likely to be offsetting benefits which are difficult to measure. For example, the program in Taiwan is recruiting progressively younger women with fewer children—so that each new acceptance prevents more births. Also, the longer a program has been in existence, the more "spin-offs" it is likely to have to private practitioners.

[3]John Wyon and John Gordon, *The Khanna Study* (Cambridge, Mass.: Harvard University Press, 1971).

[4]K. K. Kuriem, "A World Record for Ernakulum," *Hindustan Times* (New Delhi), July 29, 1971.

[5]Carl Taylor, "Population Trends in an Indian Village," *Scientific American* 223, no. 1 (July 1970), p. 106.

[6]Abdel R. Omran, "Abortion in the Demographic Transition," in Roger Revelle, et al., eds., *Rapid Population Growth, Consequences, and Policy Implications, op. cit.*

[7]"Abortion Rises 72 Percent in Six Years in Korea," *Population Chronicle* (September 1971), p. 6.

[8]Hernan Mendoza-Hoyas, "Research Studies on Abortion and Family Planning in Colombia," *Milbank Memorial Fund Quarterly* 46, no. 3 (July 1968), p. 223.

[9]*Family Planning on Five Continents*, International Planned Parenthood Federation, London, 1972.

CHAPTER V

[1]See James W. Howe, "Protectionism, American Jobs, and the Poor Countries," Communique No. 17, Overseas Development Council, October 1972.

[2]See James W. Howe, *Special Drawing Rights and Development: $10 Billion for Whom?*, Development Paper No. 9, Overseas Development Council, October 1972.

bibliography

Adelman, Irma, and Morris, Cynthia Taft. "An Anatomy of Income Distribution Patterns in Developing Nations," *Development Digest*, October 1971.

Armer, Michael, and Youtz, Robert. "Formal Education and Individual Modernity in an African Society," *American Journal of Sociology 77*, no. 4 (1971), 604-26.

Berelson, Bernard. "Beyond Family Planning," *Studies in Family Planning*, no. 38 (February 1969), 1-16.

———. "The Present State of Family Planning Programs," *Studies in Family Planning*, no. 57 (September 1970), 1-11.

Berent, Jerzy. "Causes of Fertility Decline in Eastern Europe and the Soviet Union," *Population Studies 24*, no. 1 and 2 (1970).

Berg, Alan. "Toward Survival: Nutrition and the Population Dilemma," *Interplay*, February 1970.

Blake, Judith. "Reproductive Ideals and Educational Attainment among White Americans, 1943-1960," *Population Studies 21*, no. 2 (1967), 159-74.

Bogue, Donald. *Principles of Demography*. New York: John Wiley & Sons, 1969.

Brown, Lester. *Seeds of Change.* New York: Praeger Publishers, 1970.

Callahan, Daniel. "Ethics and Population Limitation," *Science*, February 4, 1972.

Cardoso, Fernando H. "Industrialization, Dependency and Power in Latin America," in Kenneth W. Thompson and F. Champion Ward (eds.), *Education and Development Reconsidered*, vol. 2, 113-26. Prepared for a conference at Villa Serbelloni, Bellagio, Italy, May 3-5, 1972, sponsored by the Ford and Rockefeller Foundations.

Carleton, Robert O. "Labor Force Participation: A Stimulus to Fertility in Puerto Rico?" *Demography 2* (1965), 233-39.

Coale, Ansley. "The Decline of Fertility in Europe from the French Revolution to World War II," in S. J. Behrman, Leslie Corsa, Jr., and Ronald Freedman (eds.), *Fertility and Family Planning: A World View*. Ann Arbor: University of Michigan Press, 1969.

———, and Hoover, Edgar M. *Population Growth and Economic Development in Low-Income Countries*. Princeton: Princeton University Press, 1958.

Condé, Julien. *The Demographic Transition as Applied to Tropical Africa with Particular Reference to Health, Education and Economic Factors*. Paris: OECD Development Centre, 1971.

Coombs, Philip. "Opportunities in Nonformal Education for Rural Development," in Kenneth W. Thompson and F. Champion Ward (eds.), *Education and Development Reconsidered, op. cit.*

Daly, Herman E. "A Marxian-Malthusian View of Poverty and Development," *Population Studies 25*, no. 1 (March 1971).

DaVanzo, Julie. *The Determinants of Family Formation in Chile, 1960: An Econometric Study of Female Labor Force Participation, Marriage and Fertility Decisions*. Santa Monica: Rand Corporation, 1972.

David, Henry, and Wright, Nicholas. "Abortion Legislation: The Romanian Experience," *Studies in Family Planning 2*, no. 10 (1971).

Davis, Kingsley. "Population Policy: Will Current Programs Succeed?" *Science*, November 1967, 730-39.

De Tray, Dennis. *An Economic Analysis of Quantity-Quality Substitution in Household Fertility Decisions*. Santa Monica: Rand Corporation, 1970.

———. *The Interaction Between Parent Investment in Children and Family Size: An Economic Analysis*. Santa Monica: Rand Corporation, 1972.

Easterlin, Richard. "Toward a Socio-Economic Theory of Fertility: A Survey of Recent Research on Economic Factors on American Fertility," in S. J. Behrman, Leslie Corsa, Jr., and Ronald Freedman (eds.), *Fertility and Family Planning: A World View*. Ann Arbor: University of Michigan Press, 1969.

Frederiksen, Harald. "Feedbacks in Economic and Demographic Transition," *Science* 166, November 14, 1969, 837-47.

Freedman, Deborah S. "The Relation of Economic Status to Fertility," *American Economic Review* 53 (June 1963), 414-26.

Freedman, Ronald. "The Transition from High to Low Fertility: Challenge to Demographers," *Population Index* 31, no. 4 (October 1965).

————. "Norms for Family Size in Underdeveloped Areas," *Proceedings of the Royal Society*, B, vol. 159, 1963, 220-45.

————, and Coombs, Lolagene. "Economic Considerations in Family Growth Decisions," *Population Studies* 20, no. 2 (1966), 197-222.

Friedlander, Stanley, and Silver, Morris. "A Quantitative Study of the Determinants of Fertility Behavior," *Demography* 4, no. 1 (1967), 30-70.

Grant, James P. "Accelerating Progress Through Social Justice," *International Development Review* 14, no. 3 (1972).

Hanna, Willard. "The Republic of Singapore: Population Review 1970," *American University Fieldstaff Reports*, Southeast Asia Series 19, no. 5 (1970).

ul Haq, Mahbub. "Employment in the 1970's: A New Perspective," *International Development Review* 13, no. 4 (1971).

Harman, Alvin. *Fertility and Economic Behavior of Families in the Philippines*. Santa Monica: Rand Corporation, 1970.

Heer, David. "Economic Development and Fertility," *Demography* 1966, 423-44.

————, and May, David. "Son Survivorship Motivation and Family Size in India: A Computer Simulation," *Population Studies* 22, no. 2 (1968).

Hirschman, Albert O. "How to Divest in Latin America and Why," *Essays in International Finance*, November 1969.

Hooker, James R. "Population Planning in Rhodesia, 1971," *American University Fieldstaff Reports*, Central and Southern Africa Series 15, no. 6 (July 1971).

Howard, Lee M. *Key Problems Impeding Modernization of Developing Countries: The Health Issues*. Washington, D.C.: AID, 1970.

Howe, James W. *Distributing the Benefits of Special Drawing Rights among Nations Rich and Poor*. Occasional Paper No. 4. Washington, D.C.: Overseas Development Council, 1972.

Jackson, Sarah. *Economically Appropriate Technologies for Developing Countries: A Survey*. Occasional Paper No. 3. Washington, D.C.: Overseas Development Council, 1972.

Kirk, Dudley. "A New Demographic Transition," *Rapid Population Growth: Consequences and Policy Implications*, vol. II. Baltimore: Johns Hopkins Press, 1971. Published for the National Academy of Sciences.

Kiser, Clyde V., and Frank, Myrna E. "Factors Associated with the Low Fertility of Nonwhite Women of College Attainment," *Milbank Memorial Fund Quarterly* 45, no. 4 (1967), 427-49.

Kocher, James E. *Agricultural Development, Equity, and Fertility Decline: A Review of the Evidence*. New York: The Population Council, in preparation.

Kuznets, Simon. "Quantitative Aspects of the Economic Growth of Nations: VIII, Distribution of Income by Size," *Economic Development and Cultural Change* 2, no. 2, part II (January 1963).

Marsden, Keith. "Progressive Technologies for Developing Countries," *International Labor Review* 101, no. 5 (May 1970).

McNamara, Robert. "Address to the United Nations Conference on Trade and Development," Santiago, Chile, April 14, 1972. Washington, D.C.: International Bank for Reconstruction and Development, 1972.

Meade, James E. "Population Explosion: The Standard of Living and Social Conflict," *Economic Journal* 77, no. 306 (1967), 233-55.

Mehta, M. M. *Employment Aspects of Industrialization with Special Reference to Asia and the Far East*. Bangkok: International Labour Organization, 1970.

64

Mendoza-Hoyas, Hernan. "Research Studies on Abortion and Family Planning in Colombia," *Milbank Memorial Fund Quarterly* 46, no. 3 (July 1968).

Miro, Carmen, and Mertens, Walter. "Influences Affecting Fertility in Urban and Rural Latin America," *Milbank Memorial Fund Quarterly* 46, no. 3 (July 1968).

Mueller, Eva. "Agricultural Change and Fertility Change." Unpublished. University of Michigan Population Studies Center, 1971.

Myrdal, Gunnar. *The Challenge of World Poverty*. New York: Pantheon Books, Inc., 1970.

Namboodiri, N. Krishnan. "The Wife's Work Experience and Child Spacing," *Milbank Memorial Fund Quarterly* 42, no. 3 (1964), 65-77.

Nyerere, Julius. *Freedom and Unity*. London: Oxford University Press, 1966.

Nerlove, Marc, and Schultz, T. Paul. *Love and Life Between the Censuses: A Model of Family Decision Making in Puerto Rico, 1950-1960*. Santa Monica: Rand Corporation, 1970.

Nair, Kusum. *Blossoms in the Dust: The Human Factor in Indian Development*. New York: Frederick A. Praeger, 1961.

Olin, Ulla. "A Note on Historical Birth and Death Rates and Population Growth," in M. L. Qureshi (ed.), "Population Growth and Economic Development." Summary report of a seminar organized by the Institute of Development Economics, Karachi, Pakistan, in cooperation with the Population Council, New York, September 1959.

Omran, Abdul R. "Abortion in the Demographic Transition," in National Academy of Sciences, *Rapid Population Growth, Consequences and Policy Implications*, vol. II. Baltimore: Johns Hopkins Press, 1971.

Orleans, Leo A. "China's Population Problems: Generation to Generation," *Foreign Service Journal*, February 1972.

_____. "Evidence from Chinese Medical Journals on Current Population Policy," *China Quarterly*, October-December 1969.

Owens, Edgar, and Shaw, Robert. *Development Reconsidered*. Lexington, Mass: D.C. Heath & Co., 1972.

Paydarfar, Ali, and Sarram, Mahmood. "Differential Fertility and Socioeconomic Status of Shirazi Women," *Journal of Marriage and the Family* 32, no. 4 (1970), 692-99.

Rainwater, Lee. *And the Poor Get Children*. New York: Quadrangle Books, Inc., 1960.

Requena, B. Mariano. "Social and Economic Correlates of Induced Abortion in Santiago, Chile," *Demography* 2 (1965), 33-49.

_____, and Monreal, Tegualda. "Evaluation of Induced Abortion Control and Family Planning Programs in Chile," *Milbank Memorial Fund Quarterly* 46, no. 3 (July 1968).

Research Triangle Institute. *Social and Economic Correlates of Family Fertility: A Survey of the Evidence*. Research Triangle Park, N.C., 1971.

_____. *Social and Economic Correlates of Family Fertility: An Updated Review of the Evidence*, by Norman H. Loewenthal and Abraham S. David. Research Triangle Park, N.C., 1972.

Revelle, Roger. "The Population Dilemma, People and Behavior," *Psychiatric Annals* 1, no. 1 (September 1971).

Rich, William. "Population Explosion: The Role of Development," Communiqué No. 16. Washington D.C.: Overseas Development Council, April 1972.

_____. "Smaller Families Through Jobs and Justice," *International Development Review* 14, no. 3 (1972).

Ridker, Ronald. "Savings Accounts for Family Planning: An Illustration from the Tea Estates of India," *Studies in Family Planning* 2, no. 7 (July 1971).

Robinson, Warren C. "Population Control and Development Strategy," *Journal of Development Studies* 5, no. 2, 104-17.

Sanders, Thomas. "Opposition to Family Planning in Latin America: The Non-Marxist Left," *American University Fieldstaff Reports*, West Coast South America Series 17, no. 5 (March 1970).

_____. "The Politics of Population in Brazil," *American University Field-staff Reports*, East Coast South America Series 15, no. 1 (April 1971).

Saunders, Lyle. "Beyond Family Planning," New York: Ford Foundation, 1970.

Schultz, T. Paul. *Demographic Conditions of Economic Development in Latin America*. Santa Monica: Rand Corporation, 1968.

_____. *Population Growth and Internal Migration in Colombia*. Santa Monica: Rand Corporation, 1969.

_____. *Effectiveness of Family Planning in Taiwan: A Methodology for Program Evaluation.* Santa Monica: Rand Corporation, 1970.

_____, and DaVanzo, Julie. *Fertility Patterns and their Determinants in the Arab Middle East*. Santa Monica: Rand Corporation, 1970.

_____. *An Economic Perspective on Population Growth*. Santa Monica: Rand Corporation, 1971.

_____. "Retrospective Evidence of a Decline of Fertility and Child Mortality in Central East Pakistan," *Demography*, August 1972.

Shaw, Robert d'A. *Jobs and Agricultural Development*. Monograph series no. 3. Washington, D.C.: Overseas Development Council, 1970.

_____. "Rethinking Economic Development," *Headline Series* 208 (December 1971). Published by the Foreign Policy Association, New York.

Simon, Julian L. "The Role of Bonuses and Persuasive Propaganda in the Reduction of Birth Rates," *Economic Development and Cultural Change* 16, no. 3 (1968).

_____. "The Effect of Income on Fertility," *Population Studies* 23 (November 1969), 327-41.

_____. "The Per Capita Income Criterion and Natality Policies in Poor Countries," *Demography* 7, no. 3 (1970), 369-78.

Snyder, Charles. "Malthus versus Marx," *Far Eastern Economic Review*, December 26, 1970.

Soedjatmoko. "Technology, Development and Culture," in Kenneth W. Thompson and F. Champion Ward (eds.), *Education and Development Reconsidered*. Prepared for a conference at Villa Serbelloni, Bellagio, Italy, May 3-5, 1972, sponsored by the Ford and Rockefeller Foundations, 1972.

Soni, Veena. *The Ernakulum Camps, An Analysis*. New Delhi: The Ford Foundation, September 1971.

Stycos, J. Mayone. "Social Class and Preferred Family Size in Peru," *American Journal of Sociology*, 1970, 651-58.

Taylor, Carl. "Population Trends in an Indian Village," *Scientific American* 223, no. 1 (July 1970).

_____. "Health and Population," *Foreign Affairs* 43, no. 3 (1965), 475-86.

_____, and Hall, Marie-Francoise. "Health, Population and Economic Development," *Science*, August 11, 1967.

Thompson, Warren S. "Population," *American Journal of Sociology* 34 (May 1929), 959-75.

Tobin, James. "On Limiting the Domain of Inequality," *Journal of Law and Economics*, October 1970.

Tuncer, Baran. "A Study of the Socio-Economic Determinants of Fertility in Turkey," Discussion Paper No. 121, Yale Economic Growth Center, August 1971.

Turnham, David. "Income Distribution: Measurement and Problems," in Andrew E. Rice (ed.), *International Development 1971: Development Targets for the 70's: Jobs and Justice*. Dobbs Ferry, N.Y.: Oceana Publications, 1972.

United Nations, Commission for Social Development. *1967 Report on the World Social Situation*. U.N. Doc. E/CN5/417, 1967.

United Nations, *Population Bulletin* 7 (1963).

Vogel, Ezra. *China as a Development Model*. To be published by the Overseas Development Council, Winter 1972-73.

Weisskoff, Richard. "Income Distribution and Economic Growth in Puerto Rico, Argentina, and Mexico," *Review of Income and Wealth*, December 1970.

Wyon, John, and Gordon, John. *The Khanna Study*. Cambridge, Mass.: Harvard University Press, 1971.

The Relationship Between Per Capita Income and the Birth Rate in 40 Developing Countries

Figure 1

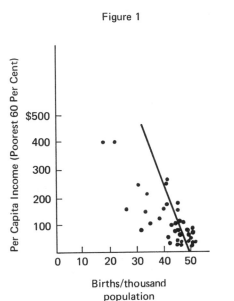

Figure 2

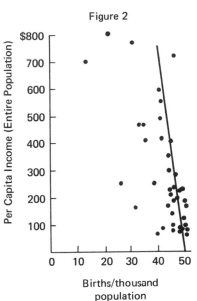

Births/thousand population

Births/thousand population

NOTE: The above scattergrams demonstrate the relationship between income distribution and the birth rate on an international scale. The relatively stronger correlation between rising incomes and reduced births in Figure 1 indicates the relatively greater importance of improving the welfare of low income groups. The relationship between per capita income and the birth rate is considered here from two perspectives. Both scattergrams represent the same group of 40 developing countries for which distribution data were available. In Figure 1, the income parameter is for the poorest 60 per cent of the population, while in Figure 2 it is per capita income for the entire population. The strength of the correlation and level of significance are represented by the following computed values for R^2 and T:

$$\text{Figure 1:} \quad R^2 = .64 \qquad T = -8.19$$

$$\text{Figure 2:} \quad R^2 = -46 \qquad T = -5.73$$

It should be noted that $T + 3.6$ is significantly different from zero at a .0005 level of confidence. When the income of the richest 20 per cent of the population was correlated with the national birth rates the strength of the correlation dropped still further. The relationship is clearly strongest and most significant for the poor population group.

SOURCES: *Income Distribution Data:* David Turnham, "Income Distribution: Measurement and Problems," in Andrew E. Rice, ed., *International Development 1971, Development Targets for the 1970's: Jobs and Justice* (Dobbs Ferry, N.Y.: Oceana Publications, 1972); Irma Adelman and Cynthia T. Morris, "An Anatomy of Income Distribution Patterns in Developing Nations," *Development Digest* (October 1971). *Income Per Capita Data: World Bank Atlas, 1971. Birth Rate Data: 1971 World Population Data Sheet* (Washington, D.C.: Population Reference Bureau, Inc., 1971).

Estimated Economic, Agricultural, and Demographic Indicators for Selected Countries

68

Country	Estimated Per Capita Income		Relative Income Inequality Total Decile Deviations From 10%	Average Annual Growth (Per Cent)			Crude Birth Rate (births/thousand)		
	Year:	Dollars:		Period:	Agricultural Output:	Population:	Period:	Beginning:	End:
(1)	(2)	(3)	(4)	(5)	(6)	(7)	(8)	(9)	(10)
S. Korea	1961	$106	38	1960-70		2.5	1950-60	45	42
	1969	210					1960-70	42	30
Japan	1961	383	45	1880-1960	1.6	1.2	1920-55	36	19
	1969	1,430							
Taiwan	1961	116	47	1920-40	4.2	2.4	1932-47	45	41
	1969	300		1950-60	4.5	3.5	1963-70	36	26
				1960-70	4.5	2.7			
Malaya	1961	368	52	1958-67		3.0	1956-70	47	32
	1969	340							
U.S.	1961			1880-1960	1.5	1.6	1880-1940	40	19
	1969								
Ceylon	1961	123	67	1958-68	3.9	2.5	1950-70	39	32
	1969	190							
China	1961	83					1950-70	43	32
Costa Rica	1961	278					1954-69	51	32
	1969	510							

Country	Year	Per capita income		Period			Period		
India	1961	70		1920-40	0.2	1.0	1920-40	46	45
	1969	110		1940-50	-1.0	1.0	1950-60	43	45
				1950-60	3.5	2.0	1960-70	45	45
				1960-67	-1.0	2.5			
				1967-71	6.0	2.5			
Philippines	1961	188	74	1902-61	2.4	2.3	1960-70	45	45
	1969	210							
Thailand	1961	101	76	1952-63	4.3	2.7	1960-70	43	43
	1969	160		1959-69	7.0	3.2			
Mexico	1961	297	82	1948-55	8.4	2.5	1950-60	44	44
	1969	580		1955-70	4.0	3.2	1960-70	44	41
Brazil	1961	268	99	1950-60	4.0	3.0	1950-60	41	41
	1969	270		1960-70	4.0	3.0	1960-70	41	38

NOTE: According to James Kocher's description, columns 6 and 7 indicate no systematic relationship between the rate of population growth and whether or not food production has kept pace or exceeded population growth. Nor is there a relationship between the latter and the level of per capita income. This is true both across countries and within countries for different time periods. On the other hand, as indicated by columns 4, 9, and 10, there appears to be a rather close and consistent relationship between relative income inequality and fertility trends. The relatively greater income inequality of Ceylon as compared to other countries with comparable birth rates is offset by the well above average level of health and education provided to the entire population and by the free rice rations.

SOURCE: James Kocher, *Rural Development, Income Distribution, and Fertility Decline* (New York: The Population Council, in preparation), Table 4.1. Reprinted with premission of The Population Council.

69

Comparison of the Economies of the Philippines, Taiwan, Mexico, Brazil, and Korea[a]

		Philippines	Taiwan	Mexico	Brazil	Korea
Per capita income	1960:	$169	$176	$441	$268	$138
	1969:	$208	$334	$606	$348	$242
GNP Growth rates in 1960s		—	10%	7%	6%	9%
Annual increase in industrial jobs		—	10% (1963-69)	5.4% (1969-70)	2.8% (1966-69)	—
Unemployment and gross underemployment[b]		14.5% (1961) 15% (1968)	10% (1963) 4% (1968)	Significant and rising	10-12% (1970)	7.5% (1970)
Ratio of income controlled by top 20% of income recipients to bottom 20%[b]		12:1 (1956) 16:1 (1965)	15:1 (1953) 5:1 (1969)	10:1 (1950) 16:1 (1969)	22:1 (1960) 25:1 (1970)	— 5:1
Income improvement of poorest 20% over past 20 years[b]		Negligible	200%	Negligible	Negligible	Over 100%
Investment cost of increasing GNP by $1 in 1960s		$3.50	$2.10	$3.10	$2.80	$1.70
Exports ($ millions)	1960:	$560	$164	$831	$1,269	$5.2
	1970:	$961	$1,428	$1,402	$2,310	$835.2
Effective land reform		No	Yes	No	No	Yes

Agricultural working population per 100 hectares	71	195	35[b]	43	197
Percentage of farmers belonging to cooperatives (late 1960s)	17%	Virtually 100%	5%	28%	Virtually 100%
Yields per acre for food grains	1,145 (1968-70)	3,570	1,225	1,280	2,850
Literacy	72%	85%	76%	67%	71%
Life Expectancy	55	68	61	64	64
Infant mortality per 1,000 births	72	19	66	94	41
Rural households electrified[b]	6%	75%	–	–	27%
Consumption of electric power (kilowatt hours per person)	39 (1951) 184 (1968)	116 (1949) 745 (1968)	162 (1948) 481 (1968)	200 (1952) 390 (1966)	55 (1953) 200 (1968)
Crude birth rates (births per thousand)	– 45 (1960) 44 (1970)	41 (1947) 36 (1963)[c] 26 (1970)	44 (1950) 44 (1960) 41 (1970)	41 (1950) 41 (1960) 38 (1970)	45 (1950) 42 (1960) 30 (1970)

[a]The five countries have many differences in their backgrounds, but each has fashioned its own variant of a vigorous entrepreneurial system and has had its own special form of access to American resources and technology: Mexico via proximity, tourist earnings and access to Wall Street finance; the Philippines by special treaty and tariff relationships, large sums from the U.S. via sugar quotas, veteran payments, etc., and moderate foreign aid; and Taiwan through large amounts of U.S. military aid and supporting economic assistance until the mid-1960s. Taiwan did not begin to perform spectacularly until it made a series of major policy changes, for the rural areas in the early 1950s, and for the industrial export sector in about 1960. The same is true for Korea, whose performance bears many similarities to Taiwan and Brazil, whose growth rate went up to 10 per cent in 1970-71 after financial reforms in the late 1960s.

[b]Approximate figures.

[c]Intensive family planning program started.

ANNEX D

Fertility Levels and Social Indicators for Developing Countries of the Western Hemisphere, 1970

	Crude Birth Rate (births/thousand)		Per Capita GNP	Per Cent Literacy	Death Rate	Life Expectancy	Infant Mortality	Per Cent Accumulated Acceptors
	1970	1960						
Argentina	21	23	1,068[d]	91	8	67	56	0.6
Barbados	21	30	523('69)	92	8	65[a]	42	–
Uruguay	22	24	833	91	9	69	54	1.9
Trinidad-Tobago	23	40	890	89	6	66	37	19.6
Chile	28	35	854	84	9	61	92	11.3
Cuba	29	32	280	94	7	69	41[c]	n.a.
Costa Rica	33	48	539	84	7	65	60	17.4
Jamaica	36	42	630	82	7[c]	65	32	3.3
Brazil	37[b]	40	394	67	9[b]	64	94	1.1
Guyana	37	42	330[b]	80	7	61	43	–

Venezuela	41	46	931[d]	76	7	67	46	6.2
Mexico	42[b]	45	670	76	9[b]	61	66	1.0
Colombia	42-44	46	320	73	10	60	76	4.1
Paraguay	43[b]	41	246	74	10[b]	58	67	2.3
Peru	43[b]	46	446	61	12[b]	54	62	0.2
Bolivia	44	44	203	40	19	50	108	n.a.
Ecuador	44	47	267	68	11	52	80	1.8
El Salvador	44[b]	50	294	49	10[b]	58	63	10.5
Dominican Rep.	48[b]	49	356	65	14[b]	58	72	2.3
Honduras	49-51	49	267	45	17	49	136	5.9

[a] Average of male and female life expectancies, 1951-69.

[b] 1970 estimate.

[c] 1968 data.

[d] Income distribution in Argentina is better, and in Venezuela worse, than the average for Latin America; in Venezuela the poorer half of the population receives a smaller proportion of total income than any other country of the region. ECLA, *Income Distribution in Latin America* (U.N. Publication Sales No. E.71.II.G.2), pp. 41-61.

SOURCES: *AID Economic Data Book*, Latin America, October 5, 1972. *Selected Economic Data for the Less Developed Countries*, AID, June 1972, p. 3. *Population Program Assistance*, AID, December 1971, p. 210. *1972 World Population Data Sheet*, Population Reference Bureau, Inc. Population Table 19, *Statistical Yearbook 1971*, United Nations, p. 76. Data on percentages of accumulated acceptors are from Benjamin Viel, M.D., "Family Planning in Latin America: The Past, Present, and Future Role of IPFF," n.d., p. 8, prepared for the International Planned Parenthood Federation, Western Hemisphere Region, Inc.

⊕ publications

This is the sixth of a series of monographs published by the Overseas Development Council in the interest of adding to the general knowledge and understanding of the problems of development in the poorer nations of the world.

Monograph Number One, *Debt and Terms of Aid*, by Charles R. Frank, Jr., $1.00, postpaid.

Monograph Number Two, *Amount and Sharing of Aid*, by Jagdish N. Bhagwati, $1.50, postpaid.

Monograph Number Three, *Jobs and Agricultural Development*, by Robert d'A. Shaw, $1.00, postpaid.

Monograph Number Four, *Trade for Development*, by Harald Malmgren, $1.00, postpaid.

Monograph Number Five, *Forces for Change in Latin America: U.S. Policy Implications*, by Colin I. Bradford, Jr., $2.00, postpaid.

Monograph Number Six, *The Bankers of the Rich and the Bankers of the Poor: The Role of Export Credit in Development Finance*, by Nathaniel McKitterick and B. Jenkins Middleton, $2.00, postpaid.

Monograph Number Seven may be purchased for $2.00, postpaid.

The discount for quantity orders of a single title is: 10% for 11-50 copies; 15% for 51-100 copies; and 20% for more than 100 copies. Checks payable to the ODC should accompany all orders.

Overseas Development Council
Suite 501
1717 Massachusetts Avenue, N.W.
Washington, D. C. 20036